Rob Beckett is a *Sunday Times* bestselling author. He lives in the Kent countryside with his wife, two daughters, their dog and cat. He has written more books than he has read.

Josh Widdicombe co-hosts *The Last Leg* on Channel 4 and has been on loads of other TV programmes but doesn't like to go on about it. He lives with his wife and two children in East London as he refuses to accept he's lost his edge.

D1136469

Previous books include:

Watching Neighbours Twice a Day... by Josh Widdicombe

A Class Act by Rob Beckett

Parenting HELL

How to Cope (or Not) With Being a Parent

Rob Beckett
Josh Widdicombe

BLINK
bringing you closer

First published in the UK by Blink Publishing
An imprint of Bonnier Books UK
4th Floor, Victoria House, Bloomsbury Square, London, WC1B 4DA
Owned by Bonnier Books
Sveavägen 56, Stockholm, Sweden

Paperback – 978-1-788707-47-3
Hardback – 978-1-788707-46-6
Trade Paperback – 978-1-788707-45-9
Ebook – 978-1-788707-48-0
Audio – 978-1-788707-49-7

All rights reserved. No part of the publication may be reproduced, stored in a
retrieval system, transmitted or circulated in any form or by any means, electronic,
mechanical, photocopying, recording or otherwise, without prior permission in
writing of the publisher.

A CIP catalogue of this book is available from the British Library.

Designed by Envy Design Ltd
Illustrations © Shutterstock
Printed and bound by Clays Ltd, Elcograf S.p.A

1 3 5 7 9 10 8 6 4 2

Copyright © Rob Beckett and Josh Widdicombe, 2022

Rob Beckett and Josh Widdicombe have asserted their moral right to be
identified as the authors of this work in accordance with the Copyright,
Designs and Patents Act 1988.

Every reasonable effort has been made to trace copyright holders of material
reproduced in this book, but if any have been inadvertently overlooked the
publishers would be glad to hear from them.

By sending in questions for *Parenting Hell*, contributors have agreed that their
contribution can be edited, published and/or broadcast by Bonnier Books UK and
that they consent to the use of their limited personal information, first name, city
and county, being used in the book.

Blink Publishing is an imprint of Bonnier Books UK
www.bonnierbooks.co.uk

Contents

Josh: This book is for Rob Beckett, you could never do anything to annoy me

Rob: This book is for Adam Hills and Alex Brooker, the real stars of *The Last Leg*

Introduction

Josh: The first thing we need to make clear is that this book is not a guidebook to being a parent. As you will find if you read on, we do not know what we are doing.

Rob: As this book isn't a guidebook, we would encourage you not to take anything we say as advice or the okay to do it yourselves. We take no legal responsibility for what we say being enacted by parents. Please don't do anything we did. We really don't have a clue.

Josh: Despite this book offering no tips or guidance, we are confident if you have kids or want to have them then what follows will make your life better. Specifically, it'll reassure you that you aren't the worst parent in the world and whatever doubts you have, it could be much worse – you could be me or Rob. This is simply the story of two blokes who thought life was really easy and then had two kids each and realised it was absolutely impossible, and from what I can tell, this is the

2

experience of almost every parent. There are loads of books out there that tell you what you are doing as a parent is wrong, but this is the one that says it'll probably be all right anyway. I have a daughter and a son and Rob has two daughters to prove it. You don't need to have listened to our podcast, *Parenting Hell*, to enjoy this; you just need to know that we try our best as parents and it really isn't good enough.

Rob: Josh and I first met when we were in our twenties. Josh was this super-talented comedian with brilliantly well-crafted jokes who won all the new act competitions. I was a young gobby kid from south-east London desperate to make it in comedy – so I naturally fucking hated this funny bastard. Josh would always arrive late to gigs with this big floppy hair like a Dulux dog. He would be super-nervous and would display his nerves by manically clapping his right hand, slapping his fingertips into his palms at an incredible rate. While this bizarre action was happening, he would dip his tiny little left hand into a pint of iced water and put his wet fingers on to his face, pulse points and the back of his neck. Then this absolute mess of a bloke would go onstage and smash the gig. I couldn't understand how someone that good could get so worked up pre-show.

I've seen plenty of shit acts that should get that worried about gigging, but Josh didn't need to; he had the skills to pay the bills. That was proven when, while we were still doing gigs for £30 in Soho basements, he won a televised comedy competition called *FHM Stand-Up Hero*. The prize money was £10,000, so he basically became the Jeff Bezos of comedy overnight. I was already jealous of Josh's career success, so when he signed with the best comedy agents in the business, Off The Kerb, and became a thousandaire (that's the one below millionaire, right?), I was absolutely ravaged by green-eyed envy. We gigged together after he won the competition and I was reminded that he earned the big bucks when he walked in with a see-through Apple carrier bag containing a £2,000 MacBook Pro laptop.

Josh: Even *I* am now thinking that was the action of a total wanker.

Rob: I thought to myself, here he comes, Mr Moneybags with his glory and wares. He was also the resident compere on a Sunday at *my* local comedy club, Up the Creek, and he was doing tour support for Alan Carr, one of my favourite comedians. I fucking hated Josh back then. The worst part about it was that Josh was so humble and such a good bloke. There's nothing more sickening than wanting to hate someone and they don't give you any proper ammo to justify it. It's just your own internal frustration and demons working against you while he's in the Apple Store dropping two bags on a laptop.

Josh: Initially, I had presumed Rob was a knob, my first taste of him being a message he put on a Facebook group to say he could no longer do a gig because he had won Leicester Square Comedian of the Year and so was too much of a big shot (he denies this, but it is 100 per cent true). However, over time, I grew to think he was one of the good guys – despite the fact he ended every set by saying 'Be lucky!' like he was a Victorian chimney sweep – and was delighted every time we were put on a panel show together. Particularly as it meant I had to say

4

far less than I usually would as he would talk for the whole recording. And this was lucky as for a period we were on every show on TV together, be it *8 Out of 10 Cats* or an episode of *Mock the Week* in which Romesh Ranganathan made the insane decision to wear a red leather shirt (Romesh denies this, but it is 100 per cent true).

Rob: That is 100 per cent complete bollocks. I never put that message on a Facebook group. I'm sure I thought it and told people but never wrote it on a Facebook group. Come on, you never leave a paper trail – that's rule number one. Romesh wearing a red leather shirt is true though, but in his defence, I don't think he realised it was leather until we pointed it out before the show started, which was great for his confidence.

Josh: Particularly as he is a vegan.

Rob: Josh gave me excellent advice when I started doing panel shows, which was make sure you laugh at everything the other comedians say. That way you get used loads in the edit as they always need a shot of the comedians laughing. Most of the time the other comedians aren't laughing as they are having a panicked look at their notes to try and get the next laugh.

Josh: The reason for the existence of this book is coronavirus. Blame that guy that ate the bat. One evening about a month into lockdown, I told my wife Rose that I couldn't help with our daughter's bedtime as I needed to go downstairs to send an important work voicemail. This must have seemed unlikely in the middle of a pandemic that had cost me all my work, but for some reason she bought it and I headed to the sitting room to message a man who was still a year away from being famous for drunkenly eating chicken while wearing a bucket hat. As the first of many exclusives in this book, here is that voicemail:

Basically, what I've realised, Rob, is the only joy in my life are the WhatsApp groups where I talk to other dads about how awful the existence of lockdown with children is. It's two-fold: it's A) laughing at their existence and B) laughing about how much we hate our friends like (NAME REDACTED) who walked into town for 'something to do' like a fucking wanker. So, I was pondering this, and I thought there's a no-risk and possibly popular podcast you can do. Say it was me and you, it could be called something like 'Two Worst Dads in Lockdown', maybe with a question mark, and you could talk about your experiences in the first ten minutes, then you'd have correspondence from people who send in their awful parenting that they've done and things that have made them feel most guilty (I reckon I watched 20 episodes of Sarah & Duck *today), my screen time on my phone last week was eight hours a day – it's fucking pathetic.*

The second half of the podcast, which would only need to be half an hour, would be an interview with someone else. For instance, Jon Richardson, Romesh, Elis and Isy together, whatever, and it would be a very funny, very self-deprecating podcast in which you talk about how bad you're doing at parenting in lockdown, and you could do them pretty quickly, and you can knock them out and

*it would give us something to do in the lockdown. If it
was really successful (which it could be because I think
people would really like it and it would be really funny)
then maybe you'd do something with it afterwards, but
there would be no pressure to. I will await your thoughts
but no pressure either way; it was just something I was
pondering today.*

Rob: I was relieved to get that voicemail from Josh, to be
honest, because up until that point he had been trying to get
me to do a podcast about nerdy Wikipedia facts that I had been
trying to get out of for months.

Josh: It was a good idea, I stand by it.

Rob: It involved research and preparation, which are two
things I hate more than anything when it comes to my job,
whereas Josh gets hard for a nice bit of homework. So, Josh
was planning to do the Wikipedia facts podcast and I was
planning to let him down at the last minute, but I didn't need
to let him down because we could never find the time to do
the prep or record the dork pod because of parenting. I was
also living a double life courting Romesh and working on a
podcast with him, however that fell by the wayside as the
parenting podcast grew. I am sure Romesh and I will podcast
together someday.

Josh: No you won't; he's stringing you along, mate. He always
preferred Tom Davis.

Rob: However, I think Romesh's award-winning career and the 15 TV shows that he does will keep him busy along with his excellent podcast with Tom Davis.

Josh: Told you.

Rob: So, anyway, with the lure of zero effort and the chance to escape my children to 'work', we bought mics and 11 days after the voicemail was received, we put out the first episode of *Parenting Hell*, an interview with Katherine Ryan in which she had to explain to Josh what TikTok was.

Josh: Obviously I now know what it is – Instagram for wankers.

Rob: We had no idea what we were doing at that stage. Our first attempt was a disaster: we recorded an episode with Miles Jupp which had such bad internet delay that we never used it. We haven't seen or spoken to Miles since as we were never brave enough to contact him out of embarrassment. If you're reading, Miles (and I can tell you he won't be, as he's got five children), then we still want you on. We know how to use Zoom now, sort of.

Josh: Three years later, we are stuck together as a parenting duo for the rest of our careers. Or at least until our kids tell us to end the podcast or they will call social services. You know when you look at your partner and think, *Is this it, the person I'm going to wake up with forever?* I have that when I look at Rob Beckett on a Zoom call every Monday morning.

Rob: Josh doesn't know this, but I've started turning the screen off and I just listen to his voice. I like to imagine the pain in his eyes when he's talking about his week, just like the listeners.

Josh: When Rob and I decided to write this book, our editor asked us if we would be sitting down to write it together. The answer was 'absolutely no chance'. I spend two hours a week on a Zoom call with Rob and that is my maximum exposure. Rob and I love each other because we come from different worlds and have the opposite views on more or less everything. Rob likes *I'm a Celebrity...*, *Love Island* and bucket hats. I have some self-respect. Had we put six months aside to sit together and debate if a sentence should end with a full stop (my option) or six exclamation marks (Rob's choice), we would have ended up with no book, podcast or friendship.

Rob: Also by splitting this book up it means we only have to write half a book each rather than a whole one!!!!!!

Josh: Yeah, that as well. So that is why this book is a conversation. Between two people who on paper really shouldn't be friends.

Rob: As much as I love Josh, we do see the world in very different ways. There are two types of people in the world – loose necks and stiff necks, with me being Lieutenant Loose and Josh being Sergeant Stiff. Loose necks are relaxed and carefree legends, who occasionally lose their wallets and miss flights but what a life they are having. Whereas stiff necks are walking, talking Excel spreadsheets who plan everything in advance. They never miss a train and they know exactly what needs to be done and how to do it. I mean, I respect the stiffies – it's an efficient way to live your life – but where is the fun?

Josh: If you want to know how bad my stiff neck is, I genuinely had to write half of my chapters for this in an exercise book because using a laptop for more than 15 minutes at a time is bad for my neck. I then had to send this exercise book to a friend (who has a serviceable neck and can touch-type) to pay her to type it up.

Rob: Whereas I wrote two chapters on Joe Swash's stag do in Ibiza.

Josh: If I've learned one thing in the last few months it is that being a 39-year-old man writing in an exercise book in public is quite a weird look. If you are planning on doing this, think about what you will say when people ask you what you are up to. There is no lower moment than when a drunk Welsh rugby fan on the train to Swansea asks what you are writing in an exercise book and you panic and tell the truth, that you are writing a graphic description of your child's inability to shit during potty training.

Rob: If you want to know who has written each bit of this book, Josh's sections have his name in bold at the beginning and mine are also in bold, and are funny.

Josh: The other way you will be able to tell the difference between our bits is that Rob's will feel like they should be in capital letters as he shouts everything and will be full of references to things he has seen on E4 or TikTok, because he is desperate to convince himself he is still young and relevant.

Rob: Josh's bits will also be full of dated references like Jet from *Gladiators*, Bruce Grobbelaar and salmonella because he hasn't moved on since the 1990s. This is our book about parenting, which basically means us moaning about the hardest bits. This doesn't mean we hate parenting or hate our kids, but no one in their right minds wants to read a book in which we just keep saying how much we love our kids – those are the absolute worst type of parents. So just take it as given that we love our kids.

Josh: So much so that we have written a book about them.

Rob: The other thing this isn't is a step-by-step journey to the first years of being a parent. When we first came together to plan this book (a meeting that went so well that within an hour I had said we really should have got a three-book deal), we wrote down a list of the big things that everyone thinks stand out when you are the parent of young children: teething, crawling, walking, first words . . . And we realised we didn't have anything to say on any of them. In fact, we don't even remember a lot of them happening. Is this because we spent those first years exhausted or are we just bad people? You decide.

So, this is a book that covers subjects that we think every parent/prospective parent might be interested in reading our experiences of. And nothing about things we think are boring. For example, there is nothing here on bathing your kid because it is not funny, it is boring to do, more boring to write about and even more boring to read. We want you to laugh, so if we have nothing else funny or interesting to say about a particular subject we move on. We are parents and most of you are parents; we don't have time to waste. You can dip in and out of the book, particularly as if you are a parent of young children you will never have time to read it in one sitting. We ask nothing of you and you don't have to remember a story, plot or premise. Pick it up and read it for three minutes, laugh, the kids call you for help, put the book down, then repeat. Yes, if you are a parent of young kids, you really should have bought the audio-book; I am surprised you have made it this far, if I'm honest.

Josh: One more thing you need to know before you start reading is that if you are already bored of us (Rob) then we have good news – this book contains the thing that has been requested most over the last three years of our *Parenting Hell* podcast: interviews and contributions from the people you really care about: our wives Lou and Rose, our parents and our podcast producer Michael. We asked for your questions for them, took out the really, really weird ones and then let them answer with no influence from us. And having read the responses, we completely regret giving them a free rein. Absolutely brutal.

Rob: Thank you for reading, we hope you enjoy this book. It is dedicated to our children, who we hope will never read it.

Life Before Having a Baby

'I will continue to say "Rose was pregnant" as I think men who say "We were pregnant" are weird, creepy and not to be trusted.'

Josh: I didn't ever imagine this to be my life. Throughout my late teenage years and twenties I was sure I would never want to have a kid, I was just too edgy and cool for that kind of thing. But here I am, not just a parent but a man with a podcast about parenting, a parenting book based on the parenting podcast and no time to work on either because I'm too busy parenting. Somehow I'm not just a parent but one of those annoying ones that won't shut up about it.

Parenthood crept up on me and my (now) wife Rose, like it does on so many people, with 'planning to not have a kid' slowly being replaced with 'not planning to not have a kid' and that then being replaced with being pregnant. I won't write too much about the mechanics of Rose getting pregnant, partly because I'm not Jilly Cooper and partly because I think it is best for everyone that we get through this book without thinking about either Rob or me having sex. Although even mentioning that has sadly made me picture Rob having sex, a horrible sight – poor Lou.

The other reason I won't be dedicating paragraphs to my child-conceiving is that this book is mainly about complaining and I can never quite get on board with people moaning about having to do loads of shagging. Tell that to 16-year-old me and see if he thinks that would be a problem. Or let's be honest, 17-or 18-year-old me. Or, to be frank, 39-year-old me.

Rob: Well, Josh might not be up for talking about shagging but I definitely am. So, in the words of Josh 'stiff neck stiffy Mcstifferson, Stiffmaster Flash, Stiff of the Dump, Stiff Inge Bjørnebye, Stiffington World of Adventures, Stiffzilla, Di Stiffano, stiff and pepper chicken, San FranStiffsco, Stiffshow Bob, Stiffingbourne, Las Stiffgas' Widdicombe, I'm not gonna lie I was way more excited about trying for a baby than actually having a baby. Now look, I don't want to come across too laddie. (I'm trying my best – I didn't even make a joke about 'come across' in a chapter about having sex.) But when you're in a long-term relationship, let's face it, the banging levels out. It peaks at the start of a relationship and then finds a negotiated level once you're exclusive with each other and have announced it on social media. Sex in a relationship is very much like a Covid cases graph. An uncontrollable high peak that is totally unsustainable but gently levels off once certain restrictions have been put in place by the powers that be.

I was excited about trying for a baby for a couple of reasons; the main one is quite obvious. The second reason is that I am a big fan of turning a negative into a positive. We were very anxious about trying for a baby as we had been told it would be very difficult for us to conceive. As ever with anything to do with having children, silly fun chat can quickly turn into quite serious semi-bleak chat. Lou, who is happy with me divulging this information, has polycystic ovaries and colitis. Alongside this I was also informed by the doctor that I unfortunately have a tiny cock and no stamina. I'm joking about my penis – it's actually fucking massive. But the quack was right about my stamina. I've got the staying power of Jabba the Hutt trying to play central midfield in *Soccer Aid* with Kem from *Love Island* and Mark Wright bearing down on him.

In all seriousness, having polycystic ovaries means that it can be incredibly difficult to conceive and having colitis would make it very difficult to keep the baby even once we had conceived. An absolute double whammy of worry. So being faced with this information I tried to see the positives and informed Lou this will be great – it means we will get to have loads more date nights and alone time together. Initially she didn't share the same level of enthusiasm as me. I was just trying my best to distract and lift the mood. That is something I have always been good at, with myself and other people. However, over time I have matured and realise that distraction and mood lifting only really mask the worries and feelings. No matter how hard you try, you will have to deal with and process those thoughts and concerns. However, at the time I was a 20-something-year-old 'ignorance is bliss' nutter. Plus I had Lou. She has been my rock for years and together I felt we could do anything.

I first knew I wanted to have kids with Lou and spend the rest of my life with her when I was on a train up north for a gig. There was a couple with a two-year-old in the seats in front of me. They were all so in love and happy and I watched them and I just couldn't imagine a world where I would have that with anyone else other than Lou. I remember in that moment

I started planning on proposing to Lou. I was earning about £200 a week as a comedian travelling all over the country for £50 here and there. We lived in a shithole flat in New Cross and Lou was the main breadwinner as a secondary school teacher. She had paid the bills for a number of years, so I was in no position at all to ask someone to marry me. Miraculously, she said yes.

So now we were husband and wife and in the doctors' being told how hard it would be to get pregnant and stay pregnant. This was a huge amount of pressure on poor Lou. As far as we knew my jizz was fine. The doctor said we needed to try twice a week for a year minimum before we could get any fertility assistance. Initially Lou was demoralised about this information as you can imagine. Especially as along with the colitis and polycystic ovaries she never really had periods. Somewhere between no periods and irregular periods. Again, Lou is happy for me to share this information, and she also has her own chapter in the book, so don't you dare give me any mansplaining bullshit. So not only did the polycystic ovaries make it hard to conceive and colitis make it hard to keep the baby, we also had no idea when Lou was ovulating so we could try and time the conception. What do you do in that situation? I kept quiet and let Lou take the lead – it was her body, she had to decide what we were going to do.

So, this is what happened: Lou turned into the Terminator. A sex Terminator. Whose mission was to make whoopee with me, Robert Anthony Beckett, as much as humanly/robotically possible. My spunk was John Connor, and her sole purpose was to locate it, keep it and protect it. Now at the start of this adventure I couldn't have been happier. It was like a teenage boy's greatest fantasy coming to life. I was so happy, there were so many possibilities. Where could we do it? How many times in a day? What could I get my personal best up to? (Currently stuck at a pathetic twice.) How much money will we have to spend on lube? Now we don't need to buy condoms, will the cost even out on the spreadsheet? All these joyous ideas and thoughts were spinning around my head. I'd be greeted in the pub by my mates like a victorious spartan warrior. 'Here he is, top shagger! How many times today, Beckett?' I was on top of the world.

However, as with anything, the dream is nothing like the reality. We've all heard the stories of the lottery winners who say that the money ruined their life. Well, within a week of this sex odyssey I was fucking exhausted. It became so routine – once in the morning, once at night and once in the day if we were both at home. I had no energy left; I was a weak empty vessel walking to the train station, being blown around like a paper bag in the wind. I had nothing left inside of me.

Josh: As always with Rob I am impressed by how much he was willing to share there, and more impressed still with the medical language, it was like *Fifty Shades of Grey* written by Doctor Hilary Jones. So you can all calm down – I'm going to go with the stiff neck option, discussing the psychology rather than physiology of how we came to be parents. It was quite simple. Rose and I had been together for five years, we were in our mid-thirties and, without wanting to get too deep or poignant, what else was there for us to do with our lives? We both agreed that we couldn't just spend the rest of our lives using our weekends to mooch around the shops (remember mooching?) after going for a late breakfast in an East London cafe that only sells eggs. I'm not sure why we couldn't do those things; it just seemed to be some kind of rule. We have some friends that don't seem to be aware of this rule and, despite being in their forties, do exactly this every weekend rather than, for instance, waking up at 6am and watching 17 episodes of *Yakka Dee!* When Rose and I discuss this couple we say things like 'What are they doing with their lives?' and 'They are really missing out'. I'm confident neither of us believes these words as they leave our mouths.

Prior to having a child, my life comprised a string of activities that I had no idea would one day be completely off limits to me. If youth is wasted on the young, then being able to lie in on a hangover is wasted on the childless – they don't know how lucky they are. So as a way of looking back at the old me, can we please have a moment's silence for the things in my life that passed away when I became a parent, like that bit at an award ceremony where they show a video of people who died in the last year:

- Going for an impromptu pint
- Being able to have a shower every day
- Setting an alarm on my phone to wake me up because I fear I may sleep beyond 7am
- Going to the toilet without asking my wife to 'take over'
- Going to Glastonbury
- Having the energy to stay up for *Match of the Day*
- Getting through a conversation without discussing what Mr Tumble's really like

But then, seemingly, we decided that maybe we had too much freedom. Maybe instead we wanted absolutely no freedom at all, for the next decade. 'Isn't going out and getting drunk actually a bit tragic at the age of 36?' we would ponder. 'Surely instead we should be going to bed at 8.30pm after failing to make it through a full episode of *Antiques Roadshow*.' Then we would further the argument with the biggest lie any prospective parent tells themselves: 'I think I'm actually bored of just going out and getting drunk every weekend.' Little fact: no one is bored of going out and getting drunk. It can be tiring, it can be expensive, it can be humiliating, but it is not in any way boring. If it is boring, why is everyone smiling with their arms in the air in those photos on my child-free friends' Instagram accounts?

Maybe the reason I was surprised I was toying with fatherhood was that I was never really interested in other people's kids. But then who is? Aside from the question of who will be the next Dr Who, is there anything more tedious than other people's children? There was no more awful day when I worked in an office than when someone brought in their baby to meet everyone and you had to crowd round and say, 'Oh, he's got your nose,' even though it is impossible for a two-week-old baby to have the same nose as a 38-year-old HR assistant. Was I the only one looking around the group wondering how soon I could sidle back to my desk to look at BBC transfer gossip without it looking like I was dead inside? (How could I have been dead inside if I was that excited about Dirk Kuyt potentially signing a new contract at Liverpool?)

Worse still was when they asked if I wanted to hold their baby. 'Yes, I would love to,' I would say instead of the answer I wanted to give: 'No, I think I'll pass on holding a human being that is so fragile it still has a weird soft bit on top of its head.' Obviously I now understand why people offer for you to hold their baby. It isn't because they want you to bond with their newborn in a special moment that it will always treasure, it is because they have been holding it for the last three months and they just want a fucking break.

Rob: Now back to the 24/7 Beckett shagathon which carried on for a few months then luckily, we fell pregnant. Lou found out just before she left the house to come and see me record *Sunday Night at the Palladium*. I was doing ten minutes of stand-up to 2,000 people in one of the most iconic venues in the world. I was so nervous, and on top of that I was forced to do my set early on a tiny bit of stage because Hans Klok, a Dutch magician who was due to go on before me, was not ready. Something needed fixing with his set, and my suggestion of 'Can't you just use your magical powers to fix it?' did not go down well with Mr Klok. So, as ever in show business, the comedian is thrown to the lions. I was sent out to perform in front of the curtain because Klok was fixing his 'magical box'. I was essentially performing on a ledge right above the orchestra pit. I was trying my best but all I could hear was Hans Klok and his team hammering and drilling their set together. Lou was in the audience so I wouldn't see her until the end of the show to find out the incredible baby news.

So I was sitting in a tiny dressing room with my mate and fellow comedian Matt Forde. We were bored waiting for the show to finish. No offence, Hans Klok, but Dutch magic isn't really my bag. I'm more of a Moldovan mime kind of man. To kill the time and to celebrate playing the Palladium, me and

Matt starting drinking cans of lager we had smuggled into the venue. By the end of the show we had drunk eight cans each with no dinner. Plus my body weight had dropped down to about six stone after the months of trying for a baby. I was steaming drunk and full of post-gig adrenaline. So when poor Lou came to find me and tell me the news, we were standing at the side of the stage at the Palladium and I was way too drunk to fully understand and process the information. Then Matt poked his head around the curtain and said, 'We going for a Chinese or what?' I had arranged for me and Lou and Matt to have dinner in Chinatown right after the show. At the time of booking I didn't think we would be celebrating pregnancy news.

We were still so anxious about telling anyone due to it being so early, and the colitis we were told could affect the pregnancy so we didn't tell Matt. Matt Forde, by the way, is one of the most intelligent, articulate and sharp minds working in comedy in the UK. Easily the best political comedian in the country. He has hosted his own TV shows, performed sell-out national tours and interviewed the likes of Tony Blair, William Hague, Sir Keir Starmer, George Osborne, Ed Miliband and Nick Clegg, among other political heavyweights. Matt Forde is also a working-class bloke from Nottingham who loves pints, pies, football and shouting. When we are out together, we don't talk about politics, we get drunk and act silly. I think I remind him of home.

If I can set the scene, we are in a busy, late-night Chinese restaurant. The clientele is mainly tourists that are struggling with jet lag, quietly eating at midnight. Then in the corner are two pissheads sitting opposite a pregnant and sober woman who is making up a myriad of weird reasons as to why she can't have an alcoholic drink. Which is a waste of time as Fordey is far too drunk to notice or care. We order food and when it arrives there is no cutlery but, due to the drink, the hunger and general lack of self-respect that being drunk affords you, it meant that Fordey and I start eating chow mein with our bare hands. Noodles are slipping through our fingers as we push it into our disgusting mouths. At this point Lou quite rightly points out this is rude and disgusting and we should wait for cutlery. Now at this stage I should inform you that at the time me and Fordey had an in-joke where we would call each other 'bitch' if one of us said something we didn't like. In a jokey and exaggerated joyful delivery we would say, 'Shuuuuuut up, biiiiiiitch.' I would recommend that you listen to the audio-book to hear the delivery before you judge us. So with this 'in-joke' fresh in our minds, coupled with three hours in a dressing room together taking down 16 cans of lager, when Lou told us to stop eating noodles with our fingers we replied in unison, 'Shuuuuuut up, biiiiiiitch.'

Immediately we realised what we had done was unacceptable and rude and did that awful drunken over-apology which is way more annoying than the initial insult. Even if the insult was an in-joke that was not meant to cause offence (audiobook before judgement please, thank you). So after the apologies and a few more fistfuls of chow mein, we left the restaurant.

Now at this point we wanted some dessert. When I say 'we', I mean me and Fordey. Lou was desperate to go home by now. So we went to the shop to buy sweets and we were too drunk to do it alone, so we picked what we wanted and gave it to Lou to pay like she was our mum getting us sweets after school. Once we had secured the sugar, Lou had to put Fordey in a taxi and book one for us. In the cab home I began to sober up and sensed the world's biggest doghouse coming my way. So when people ask me when did you find out you were pregnant?, I always say at the world-famous London Palladium. Whereas the truth is I was pissed, called the mother of my child a bitch and made her buy sweets for me and my friend. Life isn't always a romantic Hollywood story.

Josh: I used to be ashamed that I was hung-over when Rose told me she was pregnant, but having read that I think I am actually the greatest father that has ever lived. As I remember it, Rose woke me at 9.30am on a Saturday morning, which at the time felt inhumanely early but now feels impossibly late. As I came to, Rose decided to open with the phrase 'Good morning, I'm pregnant'. Which you are right to think is a sentence with quite the gear shift halfway through. The whole thing was a good taster of quite how jarring waking up would be for me for the rest of the decade.

I would love to say that I got up immediately and jumped up and down on the bed like Tom Cruise on *Oprah*, but the reality was that I just lay there and said, 'What?' In my defence I was very hung-over and the news didn't have a huge amount of build-up. Usually the first few minutes of my day were spent silently checking the Twitter accounts of people I hate, not wondering if we now needed to move house because of the Ofsted reports of the schools in our area (answer: yes).

We had already agreed to go to a friend's birthday that night and so within 12 hours of the news that Rose was pregnant – NB I will continue to say 'Rose was pregnant' as I think men who say 'We were pregnant' are weird, creepy and not to be trusted – she was already faced with the greatest conundrum of the first three months of pregnancy: how do you get away with being somewhere where everyone is drinking alcohol without letting people know you are pregnant?

In this situation you have a number of options:

1. The classic and most crap option, say you are on antibiotics. I'm not sure anyone has ever said they can't drink because they are on antibiotics and been telling the truth. In fact, it is such an obvious bullshit lie that I don't think anyone has ever said they can't drink because they are on antibiotics without every single person instantly presuming them to be pregnant. Even if it is a man on antibiotics. Avoid this excuse at all costs.

2. Come up with another spurious reason you aren't drinking. Dry February? Got to get up early to do a half marathon? Converted to Islam?

3. Drink exclusively with Matt Forde as he will never notice. Not an option, he's a bit much.

4. Which leaves you with the only serious option: pretending you are drinking when you aren't.
The only good choice.

A lot of people will do this by ordering a tonic instead of a gin and tonic or going to the toilet and pouring their drink away every now and again, simple. For some reason we went with neither of these quite easy options and instead decided that both Rose and I would drink red wine, we would put the glasses next to each other on the table and then I would drink both of them with no one noticing. On one level it was the perfect plan as no one noticed this superb sleight of hand. On another level I ended up drinking eight glasses of red wine and the only thing I remember of the evening is me turning to Rose as we left and slurring, 'This is going to be a great nine months,' and her looking at me with an expression that said, 'I hope you aren't the father.'

After three months of me drinking like Keith Floyd on a stag do, we finally came to tell our friends. We were the first of our group of friends to have kids, which left us in the weird position of feeling like we had broken an unspoken agreement. Like we had sat our friends down and said, 'We have some news, we are no longer young.' We delivered the news and there was a moment's silence, before all the women hugged Rose and the men gave me awkwardly manly handshakes that neither of us were comfortable with. Then the noise died down and my friend Will said, 'So does this mean you won't be able to go to Glastonbury?' Exposing the biggest mistake we had made, not getting pregnant in one of Worthy Farm's fallow years.

Rob: Here's me thinking Josh was a lightweight, but little did I know that he was smashing back double wine on every night out. You might be wondering if we had to go through the same sort of process for Lou to get pregnant for the second time. Well, when we found out that Lou was pregnant, we'd been temporarily living at her parents' house for four months due to building work on our house. So the less said about how we conceived that time the better, to avoid some very awkward conversations at Christmas with the in-laws.

Pregnancy

*'The store up sleep thing really annoyed me
as it just doesn't work. I'm not a grizzly bear.
I can't hibernate for six months saving up
sleep for the newborn.'*

Rob: Being pregnant is very different to being near someone that is pregnant. I cannot even imagine how mental it must feel to grow another human inside your body. Plus your body completely changes shape and your hormones go off the scale. So you look different and act completely different. What a great combo – it's like being at a murder mystery dinner party for nine months. Some people absolutely love being pregnant and find it a magical experience. Lou won't mind me saying this but she did not experience the magic of pregnancy – she mainly experienced the vomit and the rage of it.

Lou suffered with horrendous morning sickness which did not help morale and any chance of a potential sunny disposition. It must be so awful. From an outsider's point of view it looked like she just had to deal with a hangover from hell every morning, but without any of the fun of being drunk the night before. Unless that is what happened and she got shit-faced every night without telling me. Maybe Lou is harbouring a dark secret, or she just had awful morning sickness for months and I should be more respectful and stop making jokes about it and accusing her of being a binge drinker when pregnant.

One of the reasons I love Lou so much is that she is a very kind and considerate person. She's sometimes too caring and should put herself first more often. She is the most genuine and chilled person in the world. But when pregnant, Lou is a very, very angry person. She freely admits it herself and will probably cover it in her own chapter. She was livid with me and almost anything that happened near her. We had one of the biggest arguments of our relationship over the best way to peel a boiled egg. I know people have their views and opinions but no one really cares about boiled eggs that much, do they?

The disagreement was so bad that even now if we are peeling dippy eggs for the girls' breakfast together, there is palpable tension as we get flashbacks to the huge row we had back in early 2015. For those interested in the two sides of the case, I, the calmer person in the kitchen, was suggesting the best way to peel a boiled egg is to place it in the egg cup, tap the top of the egg with the spoon, then use the smaller end of the spoon to slowly pick away at the shell to leave a smooth white dome to be cut off with a knife. Whereas Lou would grip the egg in the palm of her hand and squeeze her fist shut with the power and anger of a rabid chimp, then pick off the tiny shards and fragments of shell as yolk oozed out all over her hands. I am actually really nervous for her to read this as it will start an argument again. But everything I have said is true, Your Honour.

Josh: In a book of topics I feel unqualified to offer advice on, the unique stresses of pregnancy is perhaps the most offensive for me to pose as an expert on (see also childbirth and cracked nipples). Pregnancy is something that Rose went through while I stood at the side trying to help by making toast and feeling guilty. A skill which to be fair I nailed. But this isn't really my fault; short of the film *Junior* becoming a reality, toast and guilt really were all I had to give. Let's be honest, it's a pretty sweet deal being the man. For while I was standing at the toaster, Rose was going through nearly a year of complete exhaustion, agonising back pain and having to wear jeans with a weird elasticated waistband. No, thank you. Before you flick to the next chapter, however, I would like to let you know that despite my role on the sidelines, pregnancy sent me slightly insane. So this'll be a chapter worth reading.

The problem was that everything I had done in the previous 36 years of my life I had prepared for. I did the reading for all my exams, I made a spreadsheet to plan every element of our wedding, I kept abreast of the news when I used to do *Mock the Week* (until I was established on the show and really started phoning it in). While in my head I'm the kind of rock 'n' roll icon who occasionally smokes a cigarette at a festival if he's drunk (okay, a vape, I'm not Pete Doherty), in reality I'm the stiffest of the stiff necks. The kind of person that when he did *Celebrity Mastermind* made himself a fact sheet with every piece of trivia he thought would come up, and then made his wife test him on it for three weeks (Rose, of all the things in the book I am most sorry for that). Something I think we can all agree is perhaps the least rock 'n' roll thing anyone has ever done, apart from starting a podcast about being a parent.

The bad news for me was that no one had told me that the stresses of having a child couldn't be solved by learning lots of facts about it; that there never comes a point in parenting when it is useful to know that at 24 weeks your unborn child was the size of a corn on the cob (but ideally not the shape). So while other people spent their last few months of perceived freedom playing *FIFA* or drinking one last Jagerbomb, I spent my downtime reading a book that promised a 100 per cent sure-fire method to make your child sleep for 12 hours at the age of 12 weeks. And then trying to make Rose read it even though she had enough on her plate with growing a human and testing me on facts for *Celebrity Mastermind*.

I finished the book and thought, well, that's that sorted. I then opened up Microsoft Excel and noted down the key points of the book in a list, absolutely pathetic stuff from me. A couple of weeks before the birth, my friend Danny – two kids, always tired – said to me, 'Good luck getting some sleep,' and I replied, 'Don't worry, I've read this great book, she'll be sleeping 12 hours after 12 weeks.' He looked at me with a face that mixed contempt with pity, and I returned the look, thinking, you poor bastard, you've wasted your life not sleeping, you should have read the book I did. Spoiler alert: my baby didn't sleep for 12 hours after 12 weeks.

The problem was that this book I was reading made it feel like I was entering a controlled environment, a world in which the actions you input on a baby produced a set output, like a manual for a Hewlett Packard LaserJet Pro rather than for a very, very small human who literally doesn't give a shit what your book said. Let's take, for example, the key sleeping tip of this book: if your baby isn't sleeping just gently stroke their nose and they will close their eyes and drop off instantly, like holding all the buttons on an iPhone so it powers down. Well, I thought, that's that solved. What are all these tired parents complaining about? In fact, it turns out the reason they are complaining is you can't just nose-stroke a baby to sleep, otherwise everyone would be doing it every bloody night and people wouldn't be cleaning up writing bullshit books claiming to solve your sleep problems.

Rob: Lou did everything properly in pregnancy; she read ALL of the books. I read zero books which I felt really guilty about, but I tried not to beat myself up over it. I'm not the best reader when it's a book that I'm interested in, so a full book about how to look after a kid immediately sent me to sleep. There was just way too much information and I couldn't relate to it because the child hadn't arrived yet. It's like reading a book about how to fix a car when the car isn't in front of you. What's the point in that?

We did go to NCT classes together which were so fucking dull, I hated it. NCT stands for National Childbirth Trust, which is basically a course you can take in your local area to learn about childbirth and the first few weeks with the baby. It felt like being back in school. The teacher absolutely loved the power of knowing something the soon-to-be parents in her class didn't know. She was proper lording it over us. 'So, class, what would you do if you go over your baby due date and your nurse says that you should be induced?' She's sitting there, grinning smugly, waiting for our suggestions that never came. Our responses obviously never came because none of us knew the answer. Because none of us were NCT teachers or parents. Which is why we took the fucking course. We didn't know anything. If I knew those answers I wouldn't be wasting my Saturday here listening to you drone on, filling the time so you can charge more. Just fucking tell me what I need to know and how to do it and let me go home and at least watch the 5.30pm kick-off. Lou must have squeezed my leg to silently tell me to shut the fuck up every seven seconds.

Josh: There was a moment when I realised I had been a naive idiot. It was about two weeks in, it was 3am, my baby was screaming in my face and I was thinking, *But the book says that you should be asleep, which step have I missed?* Before the birth I was an expert on how to make a baby sleep, now I was re-reading the nose-stroking paragraph of the book and looking at my baby like I had the wrong model of iPhone for the instructions. Then I was shouting to Rose, 'I'm stroking the nose and nothing seems to be happening,' the shouting not really helping the situation. It was at that moment that I realised this book had taught me one key thing that I would keep with me forever in parenthood. Not how to get a baby to sleep (I'd never learn that), but that anyone who tells you something that worked for them as if it is a sure-fire thing is not to be listened to. It turns out babies, like big humans, are all different. Who knew?

Rob: Josh is spot on; all babies are different, which makes taking an NCT class before your baby arrives completely pointless. However, the one thing NCT classes are good for is meeting other people in your local area that are due to have a baby at the same time. You immediately get a WhatsApp group going, which forms a support group of like-minded parents with babies of the same age. This was invaluable because I found having a baby really lonely as your life completely changes and your friends and family are still cracking on with their lives. Having this network of new parents really helped us as we could moan about how hard it is, plus offer and ask for advice on all things newborn baby. We made some great friends that we went for walks with and play dates. You can read as many books as you want and watch as many YouTube videos as you want but nothing prepares you for looking after a baby better than actually looking after a baby. Plus all babies are different. Unless an author time-travels into the future to look after my baby, then travels back to write the book, their words are no good for me. I found talking to other parents with young babies way more helpful than advice from people with older kids, as they are actually living it rather than nostalgically looking back through rose-tinted glasses.

Josh: Everyone I knew who had a baby seemed to have made lifelong friends from their NCT groups, even Rob, and he makes a dreadful first impression with strangers. 'What are you up to this weekend?' we would ask our friends and they would reply that they couldn't possibly spare any time to see us because they were meeting their NCT friends to drink decaffeinated coffee and discuss nipple cream. In the same way that people who are in a car crash together always have a deep connection, it seemed nothing bonded people together like sitting in a church meeting room discussing how to get a baby to latch on. The only difference being that the people from the car crash usually had better anecdotes about how they met.

From my bitter tone you will not be surprised to learn that we made zero long-term friends from NCT. In fact, we didn't make any short-term ones either. Unwilling to give up the

15 Tuesday evenings that most people normally do, we did a cram course of two full days, like those people that learn to drive in a week and then are never fully confident when approaching a roundabout. Maybe I put too much pressure on it, walking in on day one knowing I had 48 hours to find a new best friend, like speed dating but with an hour discussing the aftermath of a Caesarean section. Instantly I worried that no one matched my idealised view of our new buddies. 'He has bad jeans', 'She has a Peloton T-shirt', 'He has his sunglasses hanging on his rugby shirt; in fact, he has a rugby shirt'. (This is meant as no disrespect to the people in our NCT group, who were all lovely people. And yes, I am worried they are reading. If I heard someone I was at NCT with had written a book about the experience of having a child, I would walk into a bookshop on the day of release and skip to this section. Hello if you are reading, love you guys.)

In the end there was to be no big NCT friendship group, or there was but we weren't invited. Possibly because I was too judgey about people's rugby shirts. The only concrete thing we got out of it was a WhatsApp group that for the next two months would occasionally buzz with the photos and names of newborn babies we would never meet. It is difficult enough to get to sleep with a newborn at the best of times but it doesn't help when at 4am you are woken up by the picture of the third newborn you have seen this month with the name Hector. Welcome to East London.

Rob: That's the problem with trendy East London – it's rammed with Hectors. You get to Zone 5 in south-east London and it's all Alfies and Claires. Now the plan in pregnancy is to get prepared and ready for the arrival of the baby. You want to get all your ducks in a row so that when the baby comes everything is perfect. Let me tell you something, that won't happen; no matter how much you plan and prepare you will never have everything you need. The one bit of advice I would give anyone about to have a child is 'embrace the uncertainty'. Because that's the only guarantee you get with a kid – you never know what's going to happen and most of the time you will have zero control. I think Lou and I were over-prepared for the arrival of our firstborn to our detriment. It was exhausting constantly thinking about what we might need.

I bought and built a cot in our flat in Hither Green three months before the baby was due. It just sat in the middle of the spare room taking up space for no reason. The baby didn't use that cot until it was about six or seven months old. By that time we had moved house and we changed our mind on the baby's room in the new house a couple of times. Which led to that cot being assembled three times and disassembled twice over two different properties before a child even slept in it. We did so much shopping and organising and preparing that by the time the baby came we were exhausted. You can't store up sleep before a baby arrives, but you can sit still and not move. Try and chill out as much as you can and with the confidence and belief in yourself that whatever happens in the moment you will be able to solve the problems for you and your baby. Pre-empting every possible outcome and preparing for it sent me and Lou mad. Anything you need is a trip to the 24-hour supermarket away or a couple of clicks online for next-day delivery. Having a baby is a marathon not a sprint; don't run out of puff too early.

Josh: The first sign that parenthood wasn't all going to be nose strokes and lie-ins came when the pram arrived. For some reason your pram comes completely deconstructed and in a huge box. The whole point of the pram is that it is able to go from one place to another on wheels, so surely it would be easier for everyone if they just pushed it round to your house fully made. Still, no worries, I thought, how difficult can it be? I once put together a spinny office chair, it can't be much more complicated than that. And so it was that the Sunday morning a week before Rose was due to give birth, I got the bits of our Bugaboo Bee 5 out of the box and decided to knock it together in the 20 minutes before breakfast. At midday I had managed to get two pieces connected and was watching my sixth YouTube tutorial, thinking, would it really be that bad if we just carried our baby everywhere? I texted my friend who had recommended the Bugaboo (Elis James, name and shame) and he told me he had failed so badly in building it that he had to take it to his local Halfords. Yes, Halfords, the car and bike place. Imagine that low – the man next to you is buying a new ignition coil for his Audi A8, meanwhile you're keeping your voice down so no one can hear you asking a mechanic to attach your bassinet the correct way round. Total humiliation, something I didn't have to suffer as by around 3pm on the Sunday, I worked out the perfect method to construct the pram: Rose's mum did it for me.

This allowed me the rest of the afternoon to fit our new child seat in the car. A very stressful experience in which you undertake a task for which you are totally unqualified, knowing that if you get it wrong, your child could die. Enjoy! After a humiliating morning losing a battle with a buggy, I now promised myself I would not fail with the seat and against all odds within an hour (okay, two) and with just three YouTube tutorials (okay, four) I had the seat installed. Total success apart from one small issue: despite what YouTube told me to do, I just couldn't engage the seat's swivel function, a lovely feature that assisted in getting the child in and out of the car (what an age we live in!). No matter what I did it just would not swivel and so I returned to the house to tell Rose the good news (the seat was in) and the bad news (it was going to face backwards forever). 'Of course it won't swivel,' she replied. 'We didn't buy the swivel model as you said it was a needlessly showy expense that no one needed.' By the end of the day, I was worrying I may not be quite ready for fatherhood.

Rob: I was always so jealous of the swivel function on the car seat as it looked so futuristic. The child's car seat industry has changed dramatically in the last 20 years. Which leads to some of the advice you would get from the older generations being terrifyingly hilarious. I was talking to my dad about car seats and he said, 'When you were little we would just pop you in the footwell in your Moses basket.' Imagine if I did that now?! Someone would take a photo, it would go viral and I would be cancelled. I would have to do a podcast apology episode with Josh asking me serious questions. I'd wear dark clothes and have to look shameful on *The One Show* apologising to Alex Jones and Ronan Keating.

The most annoying thing when your partner is pregnant is new parents with a two-month-old who instantly become the experts in parenting. Giving you the fear spiel, 'Oh, you just wait; get your sleep in now as it's going to be so hard when the baby comes; you don't know how easy you've got it.' Me and Lou just sat there in silence but both thinking the same thought: *Why don't you fuck off and shut up, you sanctimonious smug cow!* I hate people like that. Even if they are correct we don't need to know about it now. Let us sit here in oblivious bliss. One thing expecting parents don't need any more of is anxiety. We have more than enough anxiety swirling around our heads without an update about how much worse it's going to get from the doom squad. The store up sleep thing really annoyed me as it just doesn't work. I'm not a grizzly bear. I can't hibernate for six months saving up sleep for the newborn. Stop telling me to do something that's impossible. I'd love a bigger dick, but staring at it and shouting at it to get bigger doesn't work. Trust me I've tried, in a number of different languages, just in case my dick is Spanish.

Josh: As the due date approaches your friends begin to get in touch, usually for one of two reasons. The first is to ask if you have had the baby yet, the most annoying text you will ever receive. Surely, there are only two possible reasons if they haven't heard from you: either you haven't had it or you have but you don't value them enough to tell them, 'Yes, Mum, they were born last week and you mean so little to me that I decided against telling you.' If you have a friend that is having a baby, leave them alone; they don't want to hear from you, they are too busy failing to make a car seat swivel.

The second reason why people get in touch – which is only slightly less annoying – is to tell you that you should use these last few weeks to do things you won't get the chance to do once you have kids. 'Why not go for dinner or go to the cinema?

You'll appreciate it when you can't do it any more,' they will tell you. I am here to tell you, you won't appreciate it. It will not cushion the blow. Because the moment the baby arrives, nothing that went before makes any difference. No one is standing holding a crying baby at 4am thinking, do you know what makes this okay? The fact I went to see *Operation Mincemeat* at the Odeon a couple of weeks before they were born. Yes, he may be screaming in my face and I may feel like it'll never end, but at least I had that lovely meal in Wahaca. I look forward to going there again in around four years' time. No, if you are anything like me, all you are thinking is, *Am I stroking this nose wrong?* while your phone bleeps with a picture of another newborn from a parent whom you took an instant dislike to because they wore a jumper tied around their shoulders.

Birth

'A big pair of scissors were given to me like I was Kerry Katona officially opening a new branch of Iceland in Warrington.'

Rob: Now parents will already know this but it might be new information for some readers: believe it or not, the labour and birthing of a child is much harder for the father than the mother. Let me explain . . .

I am obviously winding you up. I just wanted to see how angry I could make the female readership in one sentence. For example, Lou, when reading this book, didn't even read as far as the line, 'I am obviously winding you up' that follows. She stopped at 'Let me explain …', marched up to me, put the page in front of my face and said, 'Go on then, explain, you little fucking dweeb.' I can't even comprehend and understand how hard and difficult squeezing another human out of your body can be. I was in complete awe of Lou and the amazing midwives.

Josh: The day your child is born is the greatest day of your life. There, someone needed to say it before we could discount it as total bullshit. Because, really, is it the best day of your life? On the best day of your life would you stand at the side of an operating theatre while a man cuts your wife open with scissors? Would you see your wife in more pain than you believed possible? Would you stay up until 5am and then sleep on a chair? The best days of your life are when your child interacts with you, tells you they love you or surprises you with a strange phrase you didn't know they knew that instantly breaks your heart (how is a four-year-old saying 'you win some you lose some'?). Not when they are removed from another human being you love in a terrifying emergency operation.

Rob: Being the father during the birth of your child, the experience can best be described as 'a spare prick at a wedding'. You are ultimately the useless grinning idiot that is to blame for all this carnage. I hated the births of our kids. I'm a very anxious man at times that likes to be in control. I had zero control and could do nothing to help Lou and the kids and it was a brutal feeling being so helpless when you love someone so much.

Josh: It says a lot about my ability to project big worries on to minor issues that the thing I was most stressed about in the week before the big day was my job preparing a playlist for the birth. Yes, as the father I wasn't just charged with offering moral support and talking about breathing in a patronising manner but I also needed to DJ at the same time. Initially I was excited by this – I pride myself on nothing more deeply than my hugely cool music taste (I own four grime albums!) – but as time ticked on, I started to feel this job was too much pressure to put on a man who can't spin a seat let alone a record. How was I meant to find music that would go down well with me, Rose, ten hospital staff and (at the latter stages) a one-minute-old? I didn't want to be spending the birth of my first child worrying that I failed to match the beats between George Harrison and Hot Chip or that the midwife doesn't like 'You Can Call Me Al' by Paul Simon (although, frankly, if she doesn't like it she's an idiot). In the end I didn't need to worry, one of the few upsides of emergency Caesareans is that people have bigger shit on their minds than if someone has popped the stereo on. (Side note: for the birth of my second child I was presented with the same problem and ducked it by just asking them to put on Magic FM. Like we were at the dentist. My son was born to the soothing sounds of an advert for Bensons for Beds.)

Beyond my worries about being the maternity ward's answer to Grandmaster Flash, perhaps the greatest example that we didn't really understand how the birth of our child would play out was just how important we believed the contents of our hospital bag to be. 'Do you think we will be fine with just the 16 bags of Mini Cheddars and seven bags of Percy Pig Phizzy Pigtails to get us through 48 hours?' we pondered, before adding in six packs of Popchips just to make sure. It felt less like we were going to a hospital to experience childbirth and more like we were going to a school friend's house to have our first sleepover. I am confident when Ranulph Fiennes walked to the South Pole he put less thought into the food he was packing than we did for our overnight stay in a hospital with its own branch of Costa Coffee.

Beyond packing enough Mini Cheddars to cater for a school trip to the Eden Project, the most shameful item I put in the hospital bag was a copy of Charles Dickens's *Great*

Expectations. A book I had failed to read since purchasing it a decade earlier. This is finally the time I would be able to make some progress with it, I thought to myself, picturing Rose breastfeeding in bed while I looked out of the window, thought about the majesty of life and read Dickens's master work. Not for the first time in this book, I would like to be clear that I am a thick idiot. It turns out if you didn't make time to read *Great Expectations* in the first 35 years of your life, you missed the window; it ain't happening, buddy.

Rob: Luckily for me I have never planned to read *Great Expectations* so I don't feel like a failure on that front. I was a bit younger than Josh at 29 when our first child was born and my mental health and anxiety were all over the shop. My brain was a war zone. I couldn't think straight, I had so many worries and problems swirling around my head. General day-to-day life stuff and work were almost too much. Now I was becoming a dad it was like chucking a grenade into a bonfire. If we were to have children now I would be a lot calmer and assured, but back then it was a nightmare. So if you are expecting a baby and have always been anxious, the next nine months is a great time to do some therapy or some reading on CBT to find coping strategies and techniques.

When we arrived at the hospital, Lou's waters broke in the reception. Her trousers were soaking wet so, for some reason that still bemuses me now, I stripped to my pants and gave her my tracksuit bottoms. So I was standing in the middle of the hospital in my pants, socks, trainers and T-shirt. Lou obviously didn't need my Kappa tracksuit bottoms as there was a baby trying to escape from her vagina. No one has ever had their waters break and then 'got dressed' to give birth. But I had no time for logic – I was in pure panic mode.

At that moment I discovered that I'd left the red baby book at home. The only job I had was to remember the red baby book. The red baby book is this stupid little red book that the midwife at your local GP surgery uses to document the pregnancy. BY HAND WITH A PEN ON PAPER. This book is extremely important as it needs to be handed to the midwives at the hospital so they know if there are any issues or problems they need to be made aware of. But I had failed that mission. I had left this VERY IMPORTANT book at home, a 15-minute drive away. Now I love the NHS and don't want to be too critical, but surely we could get a fucking Google Doc on the go or some kind of online system? Nope, it's just a paper book with human handwriting in it. My daughter was born in 2015, three years after the London Olympics. They managed to get the Queen to parachute into the Olympic Stadium, but three years on we are keeping tabs on a pregnancy in a handwritten book like fucking Victorians.

I sprinted out of the hospital to my car to collect the red book. I hopped into our Nissan Micra and put the pedal to the metal. I drove home dangerously fast, so quickly that when I connected with a speed bump in the road I was bounced so high out of my seat that my head popped out of the sun roof and for a brief moment I could see the road with my head out of the sun roof like a giraffe driving the car. I got home in record time and grabbed the VERY IMPORTANT handwritten red book and sped back to the hospital. In my haste to return I forgot to grab any trousers so I returned back to the hospital in my pants but with the red book. I found Lou in a side room near the labour ward as the ward itself was busy and the doctor had said that Lou was only in the early stages of labour. I found my donated tracksuit bottoms that a hospital gown-sporting Lou did not need any more.

It turned out Lou wasn't in the early stages of labour, she was in full-blown labour. Lou went from 2cm to 10cm dilated in two hours, then fired out our daughter after one hour of pushing with zero pain relief. Not even a paracetamol. I don't know how she did it; the pain must have been insane. At the end of this onslaught, which I just stood watching motionless with nothing to offer like the cardboard cut-out of a policeman in Poundland, I was invited to cut the umbilical cord. The life-giving magical connection between a mother and her baby. For nine long months that had been feeding and keeping our little baby alive. But now it was time for this silly bastard to ride into town for the big moment. My wife had been incredible; the midwives had been incredible. I had done nothing. Until now. A big pair of scissors were given to me like I was Kerry Katona officially opening a new branch of Iceland in Warrington. I cut the cord. It was fucking disgusting. Have you ever cut human flesh with scissors? Of course you haven't. I don't even cut my pizza with scissors even though it's much easier. It just doesn't feel right. There was no magical moment – it felt like I was an extra in *Casualty*.

Josh: We were planning a hypnobirth, which involves controlling your breathing and mind to relax and minimise pain. In preparation for this, in the two months before the birth, each night we went to sleep listening to a tape that told us (mainly Rose) to 'take deep breaths, relax' and prepare to 'let your perineum unfold like a flower in springtime'. This was not an accurate description of what we were about to experience. As Mike Tyson said, 'Everyone has a plan until they get punched in the face.' Although I am not sure he was discussing hypnobirthing.

Rose was eventually induced on a Saturday morning, ten days after we had originally been expecting my daughter to show up. This may seem late but my mum claims I was born three weeks overdue. While this doesn't seem true, it is difficult for me to argue as I don't remember much about it, so I'm going to have to take her word for it.

Perhaps the strangest thing about being induced is being given that date for the birth and putting it in your diary like it is a task. Thursday, pay council tax. Friday, dental hygienist. Saturday, become a father. We arrived at the hospital at 10am and a pessary was applied to Rose to begin the process. Then nothing happened. In my mind, birth was all screaming and sweating and crying, but it turned out it was just more waiting. 'You have hours,' they told us and suddenly we found ourselves sitting in a nearby cafe having breakfast, even though we had brought 38 different snacks with us. It was a strange twilight zone where on the one hand our child had begun to be born an hour before, but on the other we were annoyed that we didn't have enough baked beans because they had been given to us in a ramekin.

All I really remember from the rest of this endless day was occasionally heading back to the hospital only to be told nothing had happened and so we might as well piss off for another two hours (not their exact words). Despite this, we tried to keep the magic of the day alive, using our free time to buy a newspaper to keep for our daughter as a memento of the day of her birth. A lovely idea, slightly ruined by the fact that newspapers tend to lead with bleak headlines about the worst things happening in the world. What joy that will bring to her in the future as we hand over a newspaper telling her that on the day of her birth an earthquake was killing 364 people.

Twelve hours into our birthing experience, as *Match of the Day* came on the TV, we were still no nearer to having a daughter. In fact, I was beginning to think this would never actually happen, Rose would simply be pregnant forever in the same way I can't shift the verruca on my left foot (DM me if you have any tips). I began to wonder if you could return a pram that you had already constructed.

Then at 4am (4am!) everything changed. The contractions got so bad that we weren't just moving to the next stage, but that next stage was an emergency Caesarean. This didn't sound good – nothing positive has ever happened in an emergency – maybe if they want people to worry less they should call it a surprise C-section, like a 40th birthday party.

When they said emergency Caesarean I presumed I had misheard. Surely there was a few stages we'd missed out here? How were we at *emergency* C-section? The last stage was watching Burnley v Man City. This was the first time I realised a simple truth that I would return to time and again – in parenting the line between boring and terrifying is wafer-thin. And, actually, boring isn't that bad after all. It gives you a chance to read *Great Expectations* (not that you do).

The next hours I just remember in moments. Huge emotional snapshots of the most terrifying experience of our lives. Before I know it, I am putting on scrubs for the first time in my life.

Then Rose is being wheeled on a bed down a hospital corridor surrounded by people. I feel like I'm in an American medical drama, the Hollywood edge being undermined by the fact I keep tripping over the baggy trousers of the scrubs that are at least a foot too long for my legs. Then we are in the theatre and I am holding Rose's hand to keep her calm, but I'm shaking and shaking so if anything I'm making things worse. Then I'm trying to reassure Rose I am confident everything will be okay, but we can both hear my voice is wavering in and out. Then I'm listening to people discussing the heart rate of my unborn baby and how it could drop if things don't hurry up. Then I see everyone in the theatre: it looks like a TV drama again, this time with a life-saving operation going on. And I'm sorry I keep going back to TV dramas but that is really all I could compare it to, because nothing in my life has been like this before. Maybe this is the time to repeat that a lot of people had told me this would be the best day of my life, and at this point I really hated those people. Here comes the surgeon, just enjoy it; it's magical.

Before they begin the Caesarean, everyone in the room says their name and why they are there. Pat, surgeon. Steve, anaesthetist. Josh, comedian and occasional podcaster. Why have I got such a flippant waste-of-time job? Maybe this isn't the time to worry about that. On it goes, Lucy, midwife... I have no idea why this register is happening, to make sure no one has sneaked in without a valid ticket? Is that much of an issue? I'm confident no one would be in here unless they had to be. I know I would never choose to attend one of these again.

Now a curtain goes up at Rose's waist, separating us from the imminent arrival of our daughter. And then we wait. I could really do with someone putting on Magic FM about now. All we are doing is staring at the divider, waiting for our daughter to appear. Like a high stakes version of Argos. And then, after a bit of pulling, the baby – our daughter, my first child – is suddenly raised above the curtain. Looking, it has to be said, absolutely fucking livid. I have no idea how long she was planning on staying in there, but even ten days late she is not happy about leaving.

All I feel is utter relief. Joy that all the awful terrible scenarios that had played out in my head for the last 30 minutes were just terrible hypotheticals. Best. Day. Of. Your. Life.

Rob: The birth of our second child was much more of a relaxed atmosphere. It was our second time, so my brain had calmed down a bit. We were both more confident as a couple. But, most importantly, Lou had an epidural. Now that is a magical moment. Forget the first time you see your kid, Lou's transformation from pre-epidural to post-epidural was like a miracle. I know drugs are bad, but the right drugs at the right time delivered by the right people are absolutely delicious. The second labour was much longer, but it was so much more relaxed due to the heroin or whatever it is they put in that syringe. We were also in a proper delivery room with a dedicated midwife rather than the side room madness back in 2015. I even had time to pop to the local petrol station for some snacks. I bought a picnic big enough for about nine people and also a Ferrero Rocher pyramid tower and enough Ferrero Rocher to fill it up so it looked like the ambassador's house from the TV advert. I'd always wanted a Ferrero Rocher tower and I had never seen them in the shops before. So I thought strike while the iron is hot and get it now in case you don't see it again. When I got back to Lou at the hospital, I discovered that you aren't allowed to eat when you have an epidural. So I ended up eating that whole picnic on my own in the delivery room toilet. I felt guilty eating it in front of Lou as she had contractions. Lou also politely asked, 'Why the fuck would you go and buy a Ferrero Rocher tower and five packs of Ferrero Rocher when your wife is in labour?' If I'm honest, I didn't really have an answer to that.

Now just because Lou had an epidural I am not saying it was easy. It's still an incredibly hard and long process that had a huge impact on Lou's body. But compared to the madness of our firstborn, it was more controlled and measured. The baby came at about 3am and Lou was wheeled into a side room. Lou breastfed the baby much more successfully than with the firstborn which was a relief. The baby fed and went to sleep, then Lou went to sleep. I was standing next to the bed in a side room. There was no other bed, chair, cushion or blanket. So at 3am I looked around at my options and decided to curl up on the floor, fully clothed, and sleep on the floor like a dog.

I agree with Josh. This is what drives me mad about people saying how magical the birth of their child is. It's fucking horrible. A magical day shouldn't consist of watching your wife be injected with drugs to make her numb from the waist down, then witness her scream in agony as she pushes out another human from her own body. All the while you cannot help and there is a midwife – who is albeit lovely although essentially a stranger – but now this medically qualified stranger is in sole charge of the love of your life's vagina. Then that's followed up with sleeping rough for the night on the laminated floor of a hospital. Now you might want to call me Captain Cranky, but I'm struggling to see the magic in that scenario. Yeah, sure, I had a Ferrero Rocher tower, but that wasn't enough to tip the day into 'magical'. I've been to Disney World the actual home to the Magic Kingdom. Do you know what happens in the Magic Kingdom? You go on roller coasters, you wear Mickey ears and eat ice cream. I was in Disney for two whole weeks and I did not see anyone getting an epidural and I certainly did not see any dilated cervixes. Not one, not even back in the hotel room.

Josh: One other dad I had spoken to in the build-up had told me that the experience of birth was close to magical, adding (with a tear in his eye) that when the baby is born I needed to take my top off and hold her skin to skin, bonding instantly. While I felt it may look insane to suddenly begin to strip the moment my wife gave birth, they assured me this was the done thing and who was I to question? Maybe birth is a calm and magical experience, I thought.

So when the midwife handed me my daughter to hold, I asked, 'Shall I take my top off?'

'What?' the midwife replied.

'To go skin on skin.'

She looked at me like I had lost my mind. Like she had no frame of reference for this suggestion. Why was I saying these words? She had seen a man just watch his wife being cut open to remove his struggling unborn baby, and now he was for no reason asking to take his top off. Like Fabrizio Ravanelli celebrating a goal.

'To go skin to skin with the baby,' I clarified, fearing she thought I was using this moment to try to have crack on to her. It didn't help.

'Do you know what, it's fine,' I added, and my top remained on. A magical day.

Rob: When you have a child, before you are released back into the wild, the doctors have to check the mum as well as the baby. To make sure she's fit and healthy enough to go home. One of the stipulations is that she has to 'pass water', which is medical talk for 'have a piss'. You couldn't just walk along the river Thames, passing water. They need a sample of the yellow stuff.

Lou and I were desperate to leave the hospital as we were in a super busy ward with five other newborn babies and their parents. It was roasting hot in there and one of the other new dads was a complete prick. So loud and annoying, constantly on the phone telling people about his ugly baby. And yes, it was an ugly baby and anyone that says all babies are beautiful are normally people with ugly babies. You get some right munters but they normally grow out of it. Anyone would look rough after nine months trapped in a tiny space. Julian Assange looked like a bag of shit when he got busted out of the Ecuadorian Embassy and rightly so. It's tough to look good when you're not allowed outside. We all remember lockdown.

So anyway, Lou had a massive piss in this plastic box that they gave her to do it in. Now this box was huge like a Tupperware container that you could get a full picnic in. I'm talking four rounds of sandwiches and four full-size Scotch eggs. Lou had filled it to the brim and gave it to me. So I ended up marching around the hospital with essentially a bucket of piss, trying to find someone in charge. I eventually found a nurse. She saw the sloshing slash and said, 'Urgh, what's that?' It's quite impressive to get an 'urgh' from a nurse as they have seen almost everything that can be disgusting.

I said in a sleep-deprived state, 'It's my wife's piss.'

She said, 'Why are you showing me your wife's urine?'

I said, 'Because we were told she had to pass water in order to go home.'

She said, 'Yeah, I understand that but she's already been seen by the doctor, who has signed her off to go home.'

So I had been marching about with a bucket of piss for no reason. It turns out Lou had already spoken to the doctor and had handed me the tub of piss to be taken to the toilet and flushed. But instead, I prowled the corridors hunting nurses with the piss. Not my finest moment.

INTERLUDE 1

Rob and Josh Interview Rose

Due to what our agent would describe as 'phenomenal public demand', we have decided to include the other side of the story in this book, the views of our parents and – most excitingly – our wives. Discussing our parenting, podcasting and generally imbalanced approach to life. We asked podcast listeners to send in their questions and then allowed our subjects to answer them either as part of an interview or on paper. Here to start us off is Josh's wife, Rose, being interviewed by Josh and Rob in (due to childcare reasons) Rob's sitting room. (If you want to hear this interview as God intended, it is in the audiobook.)

Rob: Welcome, Rose, to The Book. You are sitting in a foetal position, your head in your hands, with your legs crossed. This is the smallest I've ever seen you go. How are you feeling about answering questions from the listeners?

Rose: I do feel quite small at the moment. Maybe I need to power pose it a bit. I think I'm ready to say my side of things!

Rob: Rose, this is from Alison. Do you actually find your husband funny? 'Actually' does seem to be the keyword there…

Josh: Alison obviously doesn't.

Rose: Yeah, especially when we first met.

Josh: That sounds bad. It's gone downhill.

Rose: I mean, when you've got kids it's not like you're cracking jokes at each other all day. It becomes a bit more like you are running a crèche together. And then occasionally there's moments where you laugh. Often people seem to think that being married to a comedian is them just constantly trying out material on you. Which would be awful!

Josh: Though not because of the material.

Rose: When we first met, I was working with Josh and part of the attraction was that I thought he was really funny.

Rob: You found him funny then, but has he got less funny or has he maintained? Is he funny around the house?

Rose: Yeah, we're just...

Josh: I think that's a no.

Rob: Let's take that as 'sometimes'. Right. This next question is from Zoe from Shropshire: What is the most ridiculous new dad question that Josh asked during pregnancy or in those very early days?

Rose: It was when we went to the doctors' for the first 'Oh, I'm pregnant' appointment. I don't know why you go because they're like, 'Well, have you done a pregnancy test?' 'Yes.' 'Well, you're pregnant then.' So we went through all the questions and at the end of the appointment, the doctor asked us, 'Have you got any other questions?' to which Josh replied, 'Yeah, I've actually got a verruca on my foot. Can you have a look at it?' I remember thinking, *Oh wow, he's got a question*. I was quite impressed that you were going to ask something and then he came out with the verruca.

Josh: It's so difficult to get a doctor's appointment. You're in, right? The doctor's said she's got time to hear more questions. Great! Here's one. You don't want to be having a kid while you've still got a verruca.

Rose: I also remember that you were very, very insistent about me doing my perineum massage. You said to me, 'I'll give you £100 if you do it.'

Josh: Rob, do you remember the perineum massage thing? Are you aware of this?

Rob: I don't know anything about it. I'm just amazed that Rose did it for 100 quid. What is it?

Josh: It's for preparation for birth.

Rob: So what did she have to do? What's your perineum? Is that your gooch? The bit between your bum and your bits?

Rose: Why have I talked about this? Yes. And it's so you can stretch more.

Rob: So how would one massage the perineum, Josh?

Josh: I wasn't involved in the practicalities.

Rob: But you paid a woman, your wife, to do it.

Josh: Not in front of me.

Rob: Lie there and massage the perineum. Here's 100 quid.

Rose: There are so many things that are out of your control during the pregnancy that you feel like if we do these things, these things we can control, then everything is going to be fine. We also listened to a woman talking to us every night about the hypnobirth stuff; we were religious about it. But it was all bullshit because I had to have an emergency C-section, so all of that shit went out of the way anyway.

Rob: There's so much going on. You can't control it all.

Rose: But the first time you think you can.

Josh: I was so obsessed with the birth that I didn't even consider that I was going to become a dad. And then we've got a baby. It was really weird.

Rose: That's the difference with the second one. This time, you're worrying about things like are they going to sleep? Am I going to be able to breastfeed? You don't really think about the birth. But for the first one all you can think is, 'Oh my God!' Because it's the biggest thing that's ever going to happen to you.

Rob: Okay. Next question. This one's from Sharon in Lancashire. How was Josh when you were in labour? Was he trying to crack a joke and did he look like he might faint at any time?

Rose: Oh, to be fair to you, you were good. I basically felt like I went through every different type of birth before I ended up having a C-section. I had to be induced, and that was twice…

Rob: Is induced the one where the nurse sort of…

Rose: Pops something.

Rob: It doesn't need that language because if they explained what they were going to do, I don't think anyone would agree. 'So the nurse is just going to put her fingers in there and have a little move about.' Pardon?

Rose: It's so hard. You get so probed about. I was induced, then we went for a walk. It didn't work. And then I remember coming back to the ward and bursting into tears, saying something like, 'I just want to be at home with my cats. I don't want to do this.'

Josh: Oh God, I forgot about that bit when I was writing about the birth at the start of the book. That sounds like I'm really uncaring.

Rob: You forgot about your wife bursting into tears?

Rose: But then the second time they did it, it started to work. For a while, it was all going fine. I've got really strong memories of you kind of shuffling around, being like, 'Are you okay?' And me saying, 'I'm fine. Don't touch me.' Which is quite normal, I think, for birthing women; it's like you're in the zone if you're having contractions.

Rob: There's nothing you can do as the man to help really. We're the main problem, the reason it's happening.

Rose: But then the contractions were kind of dying down and the doctors said, 'Look, you can take...' and I basically was like, 'Just give me all the drugs because this isn't happening naturally anyway, so I'll just take everything.' I think I was a bit scared of the epidural, but I took everything else. And then the contractions went mad. This often happens when you're induced – they are so, so strong. And you are physically not in the right place where your contractions are. I was waiting for a painkiller to kick in and it just didn't happen. Josh said, 'I think I should get someone.' I said, 'No, it'll happen in a minute.' Eventually he did go and they were like, 'Okay, right, I think you need to come upstairs.' And that's when I said, 'Just give me the epidural.'

I could tell that there was something amiss at this point because they were kind of in and out. And this was all in the middle of the night. They said to Josh, 'Go and sleep because you're going to be needed later on.' But I could tell they were definitely trying to distract me, though they were lovely about it. And then suddenly my obstetrician came in and said, 'Okay, right, the baby's not happy in there. We're going to have to do an emergency C-section.' He was the calmest man ever and I was absolutely fine. I didn't want to carry on doing this any more anyway. Josh was asleep, so they went and woke him up and told him, 'We're going into surgery.' And he was understandably like, 'What the fuck?' But I remember going in and you being quite nervous.

I had a reaction to the epidural where I got the shakes. I did the second time as well. So I remember the midwife saying things to you like, 'Oh, don't worry. She's fine. It's just the drugs.'

Josh: I was terrified.

Rose: She was livid to have come out. I remember they do that *Lion King* moment, and everyone laughed because they had never seen such a furious baby. She was so pissed off.

Rob: So how long was that for the first one? How long were you in labour for?

Rose: I know some people have real horror stories of having an emergency C-section. But I never tell it as a horror story. I think it was a great experience. All right, Josh is shaking his head, but...

Josh: I wouldn't say it was a great experience.

Rose: No, but I think if I was telling another woman about it, I wouldn't... Some women love to say, 'Oh, it was awful.' When you're pregnant, the amount of people who tell you absolute horror stories and you're like, 'Can you just not?' Yeah, some of it was a bit terrifying but in terms of what could have been, it was fine.

Rob: I think sometimes when you are the person in it, you are in a different headspace.

Rose: Totally.

Rob: And you've got the drugs or whatever, and your adrenaline. Whereas I think sometimes, for Josh just standing there... Though of course, I'm not saying it was worse for Josh. I want to make that clear!

Josh: I had a lot of time to think about what could go wrong.

Rose: We went in on Saturday morning and she was born Sunday morning. That's always the mad thing. People tell you about their births and they're like, 'Yeah, so I was doing that for six hours.' Before you've had a baby, you think, 'What the fuck? Six hours! I can't do anything for six hours!' But when you're there, it's like, 'Oh, right. Four hours have gone by. I have not even really thought about it.'

Rob: That's eight episodes of *EastEnders*, just pushing constantly. Next question, Rose. We've got lots of questions. You're very popular. This is from Miles Malloy.

Josh: What a name.

Rob: Great name. Here's the question. When you heard
that Josh and Rob were going to be doing a podcast
about parenting, what were your first thoughts?

Rose: There was an element of, work-wise, do we need to
add another thing in? Because he already did another
podcast. I thought it was quite interesting because
before this podcast, and actually pre having kids, he
made a decision not to really talk about his personal
life – 'I'm not going to talk about my children
because nobody wants to fucking hear about other
people's children.' So I was quite surprised that it was
a going to be a thing about parenting. Though, at the
start, it was more, 'We're just going to talk to other
people about their kids.' It wasn't, 'I'm going to tell
everyone about my fucking bins.'

Rob: How does it feel now, though? Do you find it weird
that people know about your week?

Rose: What's weird is that for my friends, it's a way of
keeping up with my life. Like my best mate, she's a
real fan of the podcast. And she'll hear about things
going on with me through it. We've both got two
kids, so you're endlessly voice noting each other, so
it's a weird other way of her being able to keep up
with what's going on. So actually, it's more weird
when I think, 'Oh, I know you and you've heard that
about me,' than strangers knowing about things that
happen to us. Another example is going to nursery,

doing the pick-up and realising that you are telling stories because you need a bit of chat. But then you think, 'Fucking hell, you've probably already heard this on the podcast.' And I'm just repeating the same boring anecdote from our lives to somebody who's probably already listened to it.

Rob: Has there been anything on the podcast that has annoyed you a little bit or you felt actually, that's not right or that's a bit wrong?

Rose: I was thinking about this and I think Josh is pretty good at giving both sides. I would say maybe him getting annoyed with me about getting stressed before going on holiday with the packing would be one, though. I was a bit like, 'Actually, go fuck yourself then,' because I was packing for everyone else. You just came in and said, 'What do I need to take?' And I was like, 'Okay, right, some pants, some swim shorts.' And then I thought, no, okay, I'm going to go and pack for the kids and you just pack for yourself.

Josh: You were stressed about packing before we even had kids, crucially.

Rose: Yeah, I know. I am a bad packer, so…

Rob: Lou packs everything. We went to America with four suitcases and came back with six. Right, another question. This isn't from the listeners, but I'm sure people want to know. How do you deal with Josh being away touring so much? Or when you've had the kids all on your own and you've been doing everything, and then he's come in at two, three in the morning and he's been working. So you know he's knackered, but you need a break. How does that work?

Rose: I don't think I'm very sympathetic actually because I'm terrible in the mornings. He is much better in the mornings. And even if Josh has got back at two or three in the morning, he'll get up. Because otherwise he has to deal with me being really annoyed that I'm up, so he just does it.

Josh: Take the hit.

Rose: I think it's hard for both of us because he's been away and there's no transition period. You come from work and then you are straight into it with the kids. I'm like, 'You're back. Can you go and do that now?' So you don't really have time to sit and gather your thoughts. It is hard and I don't know if other people have that really. I don't think I'm very sympathetic towards it. And I am willing to admit that.

Rob: He chose that job.

Rose: Yeah. And also because I've worked in a similar industry, I'm fully aware…

Rob: You know they get treated a bit well.

Rose: Oh, it is hard to be picked up by a car and have to be driven somewhere. I know that's tough.

Rob: That gets Lou. We used to argue about that. 'Well, you have an Uber.' 'You got to sit in a car for three hours coming back from Birmingham.' So is that now my socialising? That's my time off, is it?

Rose: Before you have kids, you never think you're going to get caught up in that – who's got the harder job. And then it happens – that silent battle of who's the more tired, who's got the harder job. No matter how you try to avoid that, you're like, 'You've got no fucking idea. I've been shouted out and screamed at today.' And they're like, 'Yeah, but I've been…' There was a point where you were just bouncing from job to job to job. You were at the O2 one night but I was like, 'Yeah, but our daughter's having a meltdown.' It's always there bubbling along and you can't avoid it.

Rob: And also, it can be the worst job in the world if you go on stage and die and it's impossibly hard and you feel broken. But then on some nights, if you go out and smash it…

Rose: You've got a great time. I've been there at the end of those gigs. I know what those green rooms are like. 'I've just had one drink.' Okay, all right, sure.

Rob: Next question. Do you secretly think that in an ironic twist, the reason Rob and Josh started a lockdown parenting podcast was an opportunity to get away from actual parenting?

Rose: I mean, it's not a secret, is it? Let's be honest. 'Oh, I've got to go and record.' 'Right. Okay, fine. I'll just be down here. I hope the screaming doesn't interrupt your podcast.' But I also think because it was started in lockdown, we were all going mad. At least we only had one kid at that point. When you just have the one, you don't realise how hard it is with two kids.

Rob: And in lockdown he wasn't doing as much. He could go, 'Why don't you go and watch a film for two hours and grab a nap and I take the...'

Rose: Oh, God, we never do that to each other. Swap it over and just take turns. When I look back, we never said to the other one – you go and do this for a day. I don't know what we were thinking. Give each other some fucking time! It's a bit like when you try to think what you were doing with all of that time pre-kids. I remember my mate saying to me, before we had kids, 'What do you do with your time?' She had

a kid and I was like, 'I'm really busy. I'm going for
lunch and stuff.' And you think your time is so full.
But we should have definitely given each other some
more time once we had kids.

Rob: That's something that me and Lou did and it really
helped. She'd say, 'I'll take her to the park for two
hours, and you sit here and watch that whole football
match. But then when I get back, I'm having a bath...'

Rose: Were we stressy parents?

Josh: Yeah, I think we probably were.

Rose: We were probably stressy parents because I think
maybe we needed each other there as support. We
were so bad at saying 'you go off for a bit' and
having our own time. And then I had a really rough
second pregnancy.

Josh: When I did every nursery run for three months. Too
far; that nursery is too far away.

Rose: Even when Josh would drive, I couldn't sit. I couldn't
lean back because I'd pass out. So I'd have to sit
forward in the car. It was at that age when they
wake up from a nap and it's like your child has
been overtaken by a demon. She'd go ballistic if you
woke her up. And we were really considering going
to a different nursery that we didn't have to drive

to. I think you used to do some stuff with her then because I'd have to lie down or eat or something.

Rob: You were pregnant, not that you were just being lazy, but you were actually pregnant.

Rose: I will say now that you absolutely have got to cash that stuff in. You've got to play that card because it doesn't happen again, especially when there's two around. You can't just go, I'm really sorry, I'm really tired. I'm going to have a nap. I remember a woman saying to me, 'I basically pretended that I had a craving for crispy duck through my pregnancy so I could get my husband to go and get as much crispy duck as I wanted.'

Rob: Next question. It's the Crosby's Law one. If you listen to the podcast, you'll know this question. What is your Crosby's Law, the one thing that annoys you about Josh, but won't bring up for the sake of avoiding an argument?

Rose: Josh will go and do a shop and he'll come home and just put it on the side. He'll never put it away. Things like butter and milk, it just stays there.

Josh: Yeah, I just put the bag down.

Rob: So who's doing that, then, you later or Rose?

Rose: Some kind of bag fairy.

Josh: No, I hadn't thought about that, but that is annoying.

Rob: I've got a question from me, Rob Beckett in Bromley. It's a bit of a weird question, but I think you could help. Right now, the kids are young. They don't know what's going on. But they're going to go to school and then secondary school. People, even teenagers, listen to the podcast, and their parents. How do you think the kids are going to feel when they listen back, or they're aware of the stories that are being told?

Rose: We were talking about this last night, actually.

Josh: And about once every six weeks.

Rose: Yeah, it's a 3am press conference where Josh panics in the night about it. Don't worry, we take turns. So it's not just him. But I don't think they're going to listen to it. And you're not negative about them in any way. Also, it's a really nice thing in a way, because you might not know how your parents felt about you and how important you were in their lives, and how their life basically revolved around you. So it's a lovely thing to be able to listen and say, 'God, I was so important in my dad's life.'

Rob: It feeds anxiety if you're worrying about situations that might or might not happen in seven years' time...

Rose: ...That's not happened.

Rob: Exactly. And if my kids come to me and say, 'I don't want you to do the podcast. I don't want people to talk about me.' I'll go, 'Okay, we'll have a look at the holidays you got and then you can decide if you can chip in for this fucking family with expenses. Let's see how difficult that story is for you to hear.'

Rose: Yeah. You just have to do the stuff in the moment that you think is the best thing. You can't go, 'Actually, when she's 12, this will have been a really bad idea.'

Rob: And it's all from a loving place. But I think whatever you do with teenagers is not going to be right. They'll not be happy. And if I had a recording now of my dad talking about looking after me in lockdown when I was three, I'd love it. So I think it'd be fine probably; just stop crapping on the bed.

Josh: That's the thing, they're going to hate you when they're a teenager, whatever.

Rose: You're going to be embarrassing whatever you do.

Rob: You might as well be profitably embarrassed. I've got another question, Rose. If listeners dwindled, would you be willing to divorce Josh and/or have another baby just for content?

Josh: Probably the first one.

Rob: Josh is the sort of stiff neck part of this double act: he's Simon stiff neck and I'm Lieutenant loose neck. Is that him in real life as well as how he comes across on the podcast? And also what about you? Where are you on the scale of stiff to loose?

Rose: I mean, yeah, that is him for sure. Until he's had a drink though. We were going to my cousin's wedding and he was quite nervous about it because there were going to be lots of people there he didn't know.

Josh: You don't know people, and they're going to ask you what Jimmy Carr's like.

Rob: You might have to tell them the truth.

Rose: But then we were at the reception and I thought, 'Where's Josh gone?' And Josh was buying I would say pretty much the entire room an espresso martini. Like he was…

Josh: I'm a legend.

Rose: He then decided he was going to take photos of everyone. He just went for it.

Rob: Deep down, you are loose, but the anxiety just covers it up with all the stiffness.

Josh: It's like there's no middle ground. That's the problem.

Rose: No, there isn't. Josh cannot do 'let's go and have a drink and then that's it'. It's 'I am absolutely not drinking' or 'I am drinking everything'. When I first met him, I had to convince him that he didn't need to always order doubles because he wasn't at university any more. Though I think I can get quite leery on a drink. I don't know if I'm a stiff or loose neck. What do you think?

Josh: I'd say you're both. Though I think your tastes in television are loose…

Rose: That annoys me, actually, that you are really judgemental about the TV that I watch.

Josh: She loves *Housewives*. All those…

Rose: Oh my God. My Hayu account was cancelled because his card details changed. I couldn't get into it and I was texting him while he was at work – 'Can you sort out my Hayu account?'

Rob: You're loose.

Josh: Yeah, she is.

Rob: If you get two stiffies together, you've got no chance.

First Few Weeks

'I hadn't been this terrifyingly out of my depth since I was miscategorised into the top PE group in Year 8 and had to play rugby with the whole of the first team.'

Rob: There is nothing more petrifying than walking back into your house with a newborn on your own. No doctors, no nurses and no family, just two scared and exhausted people sitting down looking at this little alien.

Josh: Our first night at home was, not to put too fine a point on it, a fucking disaster. The kind of evening that makes you yearn for the chilled-out vibe of the emergency operating theatre. At least in there the baby's welfare wasn't our responsibility.

We had coasted through our first day at home – in my mind I made a soup from scratch, something that is almost certainly a phantom memory because I'm not Hugh Fearnley-Whittingstall – and confidently set up the cot in our room ready to bed down together as a family for a long and heart-warming night's sleep. Then at around 7pm, our daughter began to cry and didn't stop.

When this was still going on at 11pm we started to worry that crying may just be her thing; she was going to cry forever.

The only time she stopped crying was when Rose would feed her. She would cry, Rose would feed her, and then the moment she stopped feeding she would start crying again (the baby, not Rose – though occasionally her as well). We repeated this pattern for five hours. If anything, every time she stopped feeding it was getting worse. What was happening? Was the feeding the problem? Was she in pain? Did she hate milk, or did she love it too much? Was this meant to happen? How the hell were we meant to know? Three days ago we had only ever looked after two aloof cats, but now we had been left to diagnose the anguish of the world's most livid baby. This was the moment it crystallised for me, that despite reading a book and attending two days of NCT, I had nothing to offer. I hadn't been this terrifyingly out of my depth since I was miscategorised into the top PE group in Year 8 and had to play rugby with the whole of the first team. (Top tip number one: run ahead of the ball – no one can ever pass to you.)

A calmer couple would have perhaps kept their nerve and realised that a new baby may just need to feed a lot. They probably wouldn't have found themselves shouting 'Fuck, fuck, fuck!!!' and googling things like 'Is it possible for a baby to cry forever?' or 'Can home-made soup kill a baby?' They certainly wouldn't have decided to spend their magical first night at home from hospital in a different local hospital. Which, somewhat predictably, was where we were headed. If at this point you think that this story is going badly for us, get ready for the next bit; it's about to really go off.

When we arrived at A&E, we took our daughter across the freezing car park and she turned blue (told you it was bad). I'm going to say it now: if you are an inexperienced parent worried about your baby not being well, that baby turning blue is very much top of the list of things you don't want to happen. I may have only been a dad for 48 hours, but even I knew when it came to babies, blue was not the colour. Was she struggling to breathe? Was she suffering with some terrible illness? No, it turned out we hadn't put her in enough clothes. It's good to get the worst piece of parenting you will ever do over with on day two. Luckily once in the hospital she defrosted and if anything, the blue thing helped us jump to the front of the queue, so it wasn't all bad.

By now of course she was neither blue nor crying; in fact, she was finally asleep. Because as any parent will know, the moment your child gets into a hospital, all symptoms instantly disappear. Leaving you to look like a total twat. The nurse tried to be polite, but the way she asked 'Is this your first child?' like she already knew the answer made us fully aware of quite how bad she thought we were doing as parents. And, to be fair, I agreed with her analysis. In many ways, it's amazing the hospital allowed us to take her home at the end of all this.

Rob: Our newborn had an eyelash on her eyeball and we both nearly had a full emotional breakdown. We nearly drove back to the hospital, although I should add the baby didn't give a shit. She wasn't blinking, crying, nothing, just sat there staring at these two nutters losing their minds. Eventually we talked ourselves down after contemplating putting the baby's face under a tap of gently flowing lukewarm water aimed at her eye but our common sense kicked in and we stopped. (I don't know where the term lukewarm for lukewarm water came from, it's a mystery. I like to think a bloke called Luke didn't like his baths too hot or too cold and the name stuck.) The eyelash drama was solved by the best treatment: time. We put the perfectly content baby down for a sleep and when she woke up, the eyelash was gone. Our bodies are pretty good at self-correcting and recovering when they're left alone – it's when our anxiety and stress-riddled brains get involved it all goes to pot.

Josh: Once our daughter had returned to her natural newborn purple, I quite enjoyed the first few weeks of parenthood. There is this strange feeling of being in your own bubble away from the real world, with no reason to keep track of time or do anything except look after your newborn. Also, you get to watch loads of *Homes Under the Hammer*. I have a terrible feeling the first three voices my daughter formed an emotional connection with were me, Rose and Dion Dublin.

The days merge into a blur of daytime TV, endless toast and unwrapping parcels that inevitably contain a stuffed rabbit. Occasionally this will be broken up by someone bringing you a home-made moussaka to eat for your next 15 dinners. You will have to pretend to be pleased as they hand over the oven dish you know you will never return and you secretly think, *but I was really looking forward to getting a Deliveroo.*

Rob: Stressed and anxiety-riddled is the best way to describe how I felt as a new parent. Not only was I worried about caring for the baby, I was always worried about my responsibilities as a husband and now father to provide for Lou and my new baby. Paternity leave is shit at the best of times; even in a full-time job you don't get much time off to spend at home. When you're self-employed, there technically is no paternity leave. You just have to make a decision on how long you are prepared to survive with earning no money. For me that was six days – I had been offered a place to appear on *Taskmaster* so I couldn't turn it down. *Taskmaster* wasn't the huge show it is now. It was in the early stages but I loved the show and it was a great opportunity for me to be on something every week.

At this point in my career I was doing all right, but I was very much at the establishing myself stage. I had only been a professional comedian for three years; I was working part-time in office jobs until then. Lou had been paying all the bills and the only reason we got a mortgage on a flat was because of her teacher salary. My earnings were not high enough or regular enough to be lent money. In one of the meetings we had with the mortgage adviser, when I was receiving the news that I wasn't successful enough to be given a mortgage – always a great thing to hear for self-esteem and confidence – I excitedly told them that I was due to be on the next series of *Mock the Week*. To which the mortgage adviser asked, 'What is that?' I attempted to explain that it is a comedy show on the TV that if you do well on can lead to other opportunities and maybe even a UK tour. To my surprise the bank didn't care that a potential one-off TV gig was on the cards. They were much more concerned by my actual income and earnings, which were something I wasn't providing. To this day it might have been the most pathetic and embarrassing thing I have ever said.

So I couldn't turn down the *Taskmaster* gig, which meant my first day of filming was six days after my baby was born. I was getting picked up in a taxi and taken to West London at 6.30am. The baby had been up all night but I managed to get some sleep in the taxi. I arrived at an outdoor running track at 8am in the middle of December. It was minus 3 degrees and I had had two hours' sleep, including the nap in the taxi. For people that haven't watched *Taskmaster*, the idea is a group of comedians are set tasks. You all do the challenges separately, they film it all, and you sit in a studio and watch back the footage, then points are awarded. My task this day was to get from the running track to a microwave under a tree in as few steps as possible. The running track was completely covered in goose shit. I don't even remember thinking about what to do. I, for no real reason at all, immediately lay on the floor and rolled. I rolled in goose shit for over 200 metres. I flipped over a railing almost snapping my spine, carried on rolling and off camera I was physically sick. That was still easier than trying to get my baby to sleep the night before. But at least I was on the telly, albeit covered in goose shit being sick next to a microwave. My word, being on TV didn't feel as special as I thought it was going to be.

Josh: Is this the best moment to mention that I won *Taskmaster Champion of Champions*, beating Rob Beckett into second place? Feels a bit crass, doesn't it? Still, looks like I have just done it anyway. Unlucky Beckett. Anyway, back to those first few days, of which I remember very little. In reality this time is just a montage of vague fragments of life, some tough, some totally mundane, all half-remembered. The first few weeks of parenting are like the 1960s: if you can remember it then you weren't there (other similarities with the 1960s: lots of drugs and no one really washes). That's why when you ask friends with children for advice about the first weeks they have nothing to offer: they can't remember which teat they favoured for a bottle or if they had a foolproof way of burping a baby.[1] Our minds have a way of blacking out the most stressful memories from our lives – that's why I can't remember anything of my one disastrous appearance on *Never Mind the Buzzcocks*.

But let's be clear, these joyful half-memories are all gleaned from the daytime. And sadly every 24 hours that daytime would end and the fear would begin for the endless, endless nights of feeding. Some people had told me they just spent their first nights with a child watching box sets and listening to podcasts and so if anything I was quite looking forward to it. Maybe *Great Expectations* was available as an audiobook? Sadly, I didn't get to find out. I don't know if my friends had mixed up looking after a newborn at 2am with getting the train to Edinburgh, but I found I had very little time to fit in *The Sopranos* or *Serial* alongside the endless crying, changing, feeding and chats about latching on and tongue tie.

Most crucially, no one had told us it would ever be this hard. I know people warn you about it being tiring, but I just imagined that meant some mornings you would have to struggle through a meeting with a coffee. I didn't imagine it would be 4am, I wouldn't have slept and I would be sitting in a darkened bedroom thinking, *I am not made for this*. Asking myself, *Am I weak?* How am I totally unable to cope with something people have been dealing with for the last 200,000 years? Particularly when for the first 199,980 years of this, they didn't even get to watch *Homes Under the Hammer*.

---

1 Answer: Of course they didn't. No one can burp a baby, it is absolutely impossible and I refuse to accept anyone has a technique that works.

Everyone had the same tip: 'You just have to nap when they do and you will be fine.' *But that is our only time to ourselves*, we would think. The only moment when we are who we used to be. So we wouldn't nap when our daughter did. Instead we would stay up in the daytime and watch another episode of *Escape to the Country* because it was 2pm and we didn't feel that bad. And then that evening we would hate ourselves for being so stupid.

So instead of asking people how to deal with it, we would just ask them when it would get better, expecting the answer to be 'Well, a week or two in'. Instead they would matter-of-factly reply with things like 'You should be getting a block of four hours' sleep after three months'. Sorry, what? Three months, are you fucking with me? That is quarter of a year. Twelve weeks. Remember when you were a kid and the six weeks of the summer holidays stretched out in front of you feeling endless? Well, imagine two of them put together in a row and instead of playing football and drinking Sunny Delight you are never asleep for more than two hours at a time and changing 12 (12!) nappies a day. And then if you make to the end of that 12 weeks your prize is four hours' sleep. It is at this point that you realise that you have been absolutely had.

Rob: If you are lucky enough to have friends and family nearby you will be overwhelmed with visitors when you first have a child. One thing that shocked me was how many cups of tea and coffee I was making. I thought I had become a dad but it seemed like I was now an intern at an office job whose main role was making hot drinks for people that were older than me.

Visitors in the first couple of weeks are difficult to manage as you want to show your baby off, but you're also exhausted and stressed. The last thing you need is an auntie turning up just as your baby has gone down for a nap. No one needs two hours of whispered small talk about your extended families' recent news stories. I don't care that Jane has gone travelling and is loving basket weaving with widows in the Ganges or that Anthony is doing really well in his degree in PE at Loughborough Uni or whatever; all I want to do is eat another pizza at 11am and pass out for two hours before the baby wakes up again.

So when you've got a newborn your socialising energy is at an all-time zero. But of course you can't stop your family coming to visit the baby so it's a really hard balance to strike. Especially for mums it's even harder as you're stressed and worried with no sleep whatsoever and your hormones are going absolutely mental. You may be experiencing the baby blues and/or full postnatal depression, not to mention physically your body is recovering from labour or a Caesarean. So all in all, it's the worst possible moment to take on a never-ending family reunion production line. The doorbell going non-stop with people arriving that you barely recognise and met only once at a wedding 15 years ago.

But don't fear, I have a solution to this problem and don't panic, new parents, you don't have to do anything. The responsibilities fall on the visitor. Now visitors of new babies, I don't want you to feel like this is a hate campaign against you. You are doing nothing wrong; you are good people just excited to see the baby. Under my new guidelines you still get to see the baby and the new parents but to make it easier for everyone, stick to these ground rules:

1. Bring your own food

Look, I've already got an extra mouth to feed in the form of a six-day-old baby. I don't need family and friends coming round smashing through my biscuits and asking for a sandwich, the greedy leeches. So en route to the house, if you're hungry take some food to eat at the newborn's house and maybe text the parents to see if they need anything.

2. Bring your own drinks

Same as above. Making cups of tea and coffee is boring and it creates mess and a thousand mugs that need washing up at the end of the day. So you have three options which are: buy a coffee en route from a coffee shop (again, text the parents to see if they want one), bring a flask which you can drink at the house, or have a dry mouth and don't fucking whinge about it.

3. Nap check

Text the parents to find out when there is a suitable time to visit. Then stick to that time. The last thing you need is a surprise doorbell ring in the middle of an afternoon nap because your bolshie Aunty Jeanette was 'just passing' and thought she would check in on the little bundle of joy. Fuck off and wait your turn, Jeanette. It's not our fault your boy Nick is 43 and still a bar rep in Ibiza with no partner or kids.

4. Don't outstay your welcome

Ideally 45 minutes or one hour tops. Any longer than that and you're a thoughtless prick.

5. Force the parents to sleep

If you and the parents are happy with you holding the baby and the parents look like they are about to die, then send them to bed. At least one of them, or ideally both – there's no point in three adults looking at a baby. If you can pull this one off, you will be a hero forever.

Your Relationship

'Your life and relationship are now like an IKEA instruction booklet. Confusing, hard work and takes two people.'

Rob: When you are married or in a long-term relationship you might decide to have a child because you love each other so much and you want to take that affection and bond to the next level. You decide to collaborate both physically and emotionally to have a family: you will be creating another life form. You will be producing another human mostly in the old school boring hetero method of having a shag, which will result in some jizz seeds being launched from a willy at some floaty belly eggs with the hope that they cling on. That's what I understood from Year 9 biology back in 1999. Obviously now there are even more ways for two people that love each other to have children and I'm all for it. Unfortunately there are plenty of children out there not getting the love, attention and care all children deserve. So the more children being loved and cared for, whoever and whatever their parents are, then that's all the better in my eyes.

So now you have your child you are excited as the plan is for it to bring you even closer together as a couple. I've got some bad news for you, readers – in the first few years it's going to drive you apart. Not because you don't love your partner any more; having a child won't ruin your relationship – it will just radically change it forever. Especially in the first four years when you aren't really a married couple any more; you are now two people running a not-for-profit charitable organisation. The charity in question solely works towards the support and care of one individual child. There is so much to do and so little time and energy that the only way to look after a child without losing your marbles is divide and conquer. If you are in a couple, tag-teaming with the childcare is the best way to succeed. When one parent is doing the night feed the other is sleeping. When one parent is taking the baby out for a walk the other parent is tidying the house. You end up doing jobs separately all the time; you even socialise separately. No couples' dinners any more as you will need a babysitter, which costs money and more importantly, needs trust. It's hard to trust a stranger to look after your baby in the early stages – as they get older, you become more relaxed. So you have separate nights out, on Friday night one of you goes out and one of you has the baby, then you swap over on the Saturday night to reverse the roles. You become ships in the night, and it's a very difficult time for the relationship.

You have to make a concerted effort to carve out couple time as that's the first thing that gets crossed out of the diary when your schedule gets busy. But even when you find the time, you're so knackered you can't be bothered. When you are with friends you have to put a brave face on it and power through the social event so you don't look rude. But with your partner you can be honest and say it how it is.

I have so much respect for single-parent families, as to raise a kid on your own must be one of the hardest things any person can do. Stick your mathematics and physics PhDs up your arse. We can all do a bit of adding up but you try working full-time and raising two kids on your own for 18 years. Having said that, there is a special bond that develops between a single parent and their child that those of us in two-parent households will never quite experience.

Josh: They say you should never go into business with friends, as suddenly all the joy of your shared interests, world view and sense of humour is replaced with petty arguments over whether it should be called *The* Facebook. It is the story of so many great bands from The Beatles to East 17: when friendship becomes a business arrangement it all goes wrong. Well, replace the word 'friendship' with 'relationship' and the phrase 'should we sack Brian Harvey for saying he took 12 Es in one night?' with 'which of us is going to change a baby's nappy on two hours' sleep?' and you will understand how becoming parents can impact a marriage.

The theory is that the way you are meant to get through this early period is by communicating with each other and being honest and open about how the whole thing is making you feel, strengthening your bond through parenting. But realistically, come on now. Who is doing that? Instead we opted to strengthen our bond as a couple by converting our lack of sleep into deep pettiness from the moment we woke up to the moment we failed to go to bed. In the hope of making you, the readers, feel better about your own lives, here is a list of minor things that have annoyed Rose and me in the last week:

- **Josh:** The fact that Rose drinks her morning cup of tea too slowly
- **Rose:** The fact that Josh gets to leave the house for work
- **Josh:** The fact that I am still having to work; it isn't like I'm leaving the house to go on a stag do
- **Rose:** The fact that Josh loses his keys three times a day and is incapable of finding anything
- **Josh:** The fact that Rose puts empty bottles of oat milk back in the fridge
- **Rose:** The fact that Josh tells me to hurry up drinking my cup of tea in the morning

Obviously now I look at these things I can see them for what they are: pointless, petty and a complete waste of everyone's time. Although, for the record, I was not rushing Rose on her morning tea and maybe she should appreciate that I let her sit in bed and drink her tea in the first place. (I'm really hoping she doesn't read this bit.)

The problem is that you are aware you are doing it but you still can't stop yourself in the moment. Perhaps one of my worst traits is that I have now developed a system where I will volunteer to do something but then silently get angry about the fact I have to do it. 'Of course I will get up and let you lie in,' I will say, like the great husband that I am before taking our children downstairs and grumbling to myself that I can't believe Rose has made me get up so she can have a lie-in. 'Why is it always me?' I will mumble, totally discounting the simple explanation that I happily volunteered to do it. (I am hoping she doesn't read this bit either.)

Rob: When me and Lou had our first child, we made a promise to never argue over who was the most tired. We said it should never be a competition, it's a team effort at all times. Cut to a month later we are both in the middle of The Glades shopping centre in Bromley, exhausted and livid with each other and our life choices. Lou was talking about how little sleep she had the night before. I replied yes, we are both very tired but like we said, let's not make this a competition. Lou stared into my dead, dark, bag-ridden eyes with her own dead, dark, bag-ridden eyes with the intensity of Paul Hollywood, but with zero sexual magnetism and said, 'It's not a competition, but if it was a competition I would win.' I decided for the sake of my health to gently nod and not reply.

Josh: Rose and I play the tiredness competition but pretend we aren't. Instead we will just both throw out facts and figures about our sleep as if it is just idle conversation, rather than what it is – a way of telling the other one you are more tired. 'Mad to think I only got back from work at 2am and I'm already up,' I will say, like I'm just making chat in the queue at Londis rather than trying to prove to my wife my life is harder than hers. 'Crazy that I didn't get up after 6.30 in the whole week you were away working,' Rose will reply. To be honest we do this so much we would be better off using the time to let each other go back to bed for a nap.

Rob: Lou and I booked a babysitter for three hours so we could have a date night a few years ago when the kids were younger. I didn't really need to explain that the kids were younger, did I? I assume anyone reading this is aware of the concept of time and how it works. Essentially if something happened a few years ago we can all accept that everyone involved was younger. Anyway, the babysitter arrived at 8pm once the kids were asleep. We left the house at 8.05pm and arrived at a local Turkish restaurant at 8.11pm. We had bread and hummus as a starter, then we each had a chicken shish kebab with one glass of wine and one bottle of beer. We finished our meal and settled the bill by 8.56pm. We sat there looking at each other, thinking, what the fuck are we supposed to do now? We didn't want dessert as we were both on a diet because of all the takeaways we had been having when it had been manic with the babies. We both certainly didn't want another drink as I was driving and one of us had to do the night feed at about 2.30am. So I suggested a slow drive back to the house with the radio on. Like a date in the Midwest of America in 1957.

After driving as slowly as I possibly could, we pulled up outside our house at 9.03pm. We had been out of the house for 58 minutes. We sat there not knowing what to do as we had booked the babysitter for three hours and she hadn't even broken the first full hour yet. In the end we drove to the supermarket to do a big shop. When we got back home we left the shopping in the boot of the car until the babysitter left so we didn't look weird.

Josh: I am impressed Rob managed to get there and back in an hour and three minutes, particularly as he lives in south-east London so would have had to travel a long way to get to a good restaurant. When this happened to us we did at least get out of the house for a whole hour, which looking back feels a real achievement.

For us it was an important night. To celebrate reaching three months of parenthood, Rose and I planned to get a babysitter and go out for dinner like we used to. Sometimes you need a dream to keep you going when you are at your lowest and this is where we were. Like a man walking through the desert imagining that one day he would find water, we would tell ourselves, 'It may be 3am and we may be yet to have a single minute's sleep, but one day in just ten weeks' time, we will be sitting together in a Pizza Express complaining that you don't get enough garlic butter per dough ball.' Dare to dream.

So when the three-month mark arrived and our daughter was ~~sleeping for 12 hours a night~~ doing just as badly as at the three-week stage, we decided that we had earned our night out. The taxi to the restaurant took us through Soho and we gazed out of the window at the carefree people drinking, smoking and talking about something that wasn't the rubber tip on feeding bottles. Suddenly we realised that for some reason the world had carried on without us. 'After dinner we should just go and have a few drinks. So what if we have to get up early, it's only one morning,' we agreed, both genuinely believing every word we said. After all, this was a big night. To give you some context of just how big, we had both had a shower.

In the taxi I told Rose that just for tonight I was putting a ban on discussing anything to do with parenthood, a pathetic and ultimately futile rule that mainly just drew attention to the lack of anything else left in our lives. I'm not sure what I imagined would happen, suddenly the moment we sat down we would forget about our child and discuss the future of the European Union and the books of Martin Amis? It seemed unlikely, as we had never discussed these things before we had a baby, so it would have been a strange time to start.

The dinner was booked for 8pm. By 8.48pm, we were done. The combination of the unfamiliar impact of the alcohol, our lack of sleep and the high carbohydrate hit of the dough balls meant that by the end of the main we were both sitting there like two exhausted heavyweight boxers waiting for the bell in the 12th round, praying the other one would do the right thing and say, 'Shall we just call it a night?' Like Rob we paid the babysitter for the extra hours to save embarrassment. I am now sure they are on to this, putting themselves forward to all new couples knowing they will do an hour's work and get treble bubble.

Rob: You know what, good luck to them; it takes a special kind of person to put themselves forward to deal with other people's children.

Josh: In contrast, perhaps the worst people in the world are those parents that tell you that having children has made them stronger as a couple, that they can now see a deeper strength and beauty to their partner because they have witnessed them look after a child. Can I speak for the nation when I say, absolutely do one. What reality are you living in? The only way parenthood makes you stronger as a couple is that you realise that if your relationship can survive this it can survive anything. Parenthood makes you stronger as a couple in the same way the Blitz made East London stronger as a place; everything may have been smashed to smithereens, but the Nazis/our babies haven't broken us.

That and it makes you value every moment where it is just the two of you. Suddenly that hour that was filler in your old life is the bit that drives you through the day, telling yourself in two hours you will be sitting on the sofa together with a curry watching *Celebrity MasterChef*. Does that frankly sad state of affairs hint that your life is now stalled at a pathetic middle age or does it show a new understanding of each other, that you don't need to be going on romantic city breaks or enjoying nights in bars drinking espresso martinis to know what you have together? I like to think it is the second of these but it is probably the first.

Rob: It's also worth adding, if you didn't already know, that you're not going have any sex for ages when you first have children. Even when you do it will be deeply average for everyone involved as both of you will be tired and sad. This doesn't last forever – our youngest is four now and Lou can't keep her hands off me! By that I mean she keeps putting her hands on me to push me away and says, 'Not tonight. I thought I texted you to book it in for Friday night?' That's right, people, you will be scheduling sexy time, and that's something you're just going to have to accept and deal with. Spur of the moment, spontaneity, heat of the moment are words and phrases that children make disappear. Your life and relationship are now like an IKEA instruction booklet. Confusing, hard work and takes two people.

Josh: It is strange the things you miss from your pre-parenthood relationship. For the first six months of having a baby the thing I missed most of all was being able to turn the light on when we went to bed, rather than having to work my way silently across the bedroom from the light of my iPhone screen (torch too much of a gamble with waking her) like I'm burgling a footballer's house on a Champions League night. Who knew one of my favourite parts of our relationship was that moment when we could wind down at the end of a long day by sitting in bed and reading books (looking at our phones)?

What this did mean was that I was hugely excited when after six months we decided the time had come to move our daughter into her own room. We were taking our old lives back. For that 15 minutes before sleep we weren't just parents but we were a couple again. We could read, we could talk, we could have… well, one step at a time.

And so with glee we moved our daughter into her own room and put her down to sleep and suddenly, somehow everything felt so hollow. I didn't feel joy or freedom, I felt sadness she had gone, that I had been so busy complaining about stubbing my toe on a cot in the dark that I hadn't appreciated the joy of having our daughter sleep next to us. I felt disloyal, like I had thrown her out of her home just so I could read Richard Osman's *The Thursday Murder Club*. And then I began to worry; maybe I didn't want to go back to the couple we used to be. I liked being parents. And before we knew it this would be over and our daughter would have left us, not for her own room but her own house. And then I thought maybe we should move her back into our room for just one more month. But Rose said no because it was an absolutely insane idea. Bloody hell, parenting, what a headfuck.

INTERLUDE 2

Lou Gets Her Say
(Finally)

Next up spilling the beans on what she thinks of her husband is Lou, answering questions from the *Parenting Hell* podcast listeners. As a former history teacher, Lou decided to answer these questions on paper, firstly as preserving the historical record is very important and also so Rob could experience what it was like to not have a right of reply.

Reagan: Do you trust Rob to be across all the info about the kids? Do you correct him if he gets something wrong or just let it slide?

Rob and I are very different when it comes to being across details and how much I correct him when he gets something wrong generally depends on how tired and petty I'm feeling. Rob very much favours a laissez-faire, 'it'll all work out in the end, you worry too much, Lou' approach, whereas I am acutely anxious all the time the girls will have the wrong uniform on, or the wrong book, or I'll get the days of clubs confused and be late for pick-up. So while I'm worrying I'm going to mentally scar the children by leaving them at school for an hour too long, Rob is his own PR machine and by the time the kids have been in the car three minutes he'll have them convinced that they're actually really lucky to spend a whole extra hour at school and it was totally on purpose. On a good day, I'll let almost anything that isn't going to cause a medical emergency slide; on a bad day, when Rob's been away for a few nights and I'm on four hours' sleep total, I will nit-pick the name of our daughter's friend's little sister that Rob has met maybe once three months ago at the end of a play date. Because it's good to keep him on his toes. What kind of wife will he get today? Who knows?

Katy, Bristol: **Rob and Josh have talked before about 'the mental load' but I'm not sure they really got it. In my house, it definitely falls to me as the mum to manage this and it's the hardest part of parenting, I think. What are your thoughts on this? Does Rob do his share?**

The mental load is a tricky one in our house. In fairness, Rob does a lot at home, and we try to share it as equally as we can. However, it's hard to be anything approaching 50/50 because of the way Rob works. So there are big chunks of time where I'm at home by myself with the girls, so obviously it falls to me to keep anything ticking over that needs consistency. Rob will pick up things when he's at home but it's hard because I do it most of the time, so it is often easier to just do it myself rather than explain what needs to be done, how to do it and why it's important. Especially as the way Rob does everything is wrong (read: not the way I'd do it). Rob also has a lot more going on with work that I don't have in my mental load so it probably balances out on the whole.

BUT – and it's a big BUT – the mental load is impossible to divide properly, or even explain to Rob, because we are at totally different ends of the spectrum of what we consider 'necessary' and 'optional' tasks, as well as our approach to when things need to be sorted out. So with things like birthday parties, Christmas presents or holiday packing, it's like we're speaking a different language. I like to be at a doomsday prepper level of organisation as I enjoy the moment more if I know I've prepared everything. Rob would quite happily take the kids on holiday without any luggage and just 'pop' to a supermarket and pick up some T-shirts as we go. Whereas that makes me physically itchy. It has taken a good few years to settle into our 'roles'. I know now trying to make him care about what's going in the girls' party bags three months in advance is a joyless endeavour. While he's learnt that telling me to 'calm down' and 'go with the flow' is going to encourage me to have an 'accident' with his Lego…

Gina, London: Is there anything Rob does that gets on your nerves but you haven't told him yet because you can't be bothered with the argument?

OOOOH, buckle up, kids, this could take a while! Do you know what? What makes Rob a brilliant dad is also what's the most infuriating sometimes: he's just so bloody fun. Which is amazing, but can also be total chaos. He's normally at his most 'fun' just before bedtime or as he is about to leave for work.

So there will be three or four half-finished board games strewn across the floor, the girls will be slathering each other in my make-up – that he's told them they are allowed to use without any discussion at all – and he will have totally unnecessarily set up the paddling pool as well. Then precisely three minutes later, he'll go, 'Right, I've got to leave in five minutes,' and I'm left there trying to persuade two gleefully feral children to get into bed while the dog chews a hole in the paddling pool.

Jodi, Littlehampton, West Sussex: What's one thing that Rob does that makes you consider murdering him in his sleep?!

I love Rob so much. He's an incredible husband and father, and he's my best friend. He's also deeply, deeply, DEEPLY annoying to live with sometimes, especially when he's well rested or not gigged for a while. My favourite Rob is halfway through a tour and starting to tire. I genuinely think our marriage works because he has an audience outside of the house. He has a need for attention that is impossible for one person to satisfy. Sometimes he says that he doesn't know where the girls get their energy from because they just go and go and go – honestly, the apple has not fallen far from the tree. For someone with such honed skills in reading a room at a gig and pitching jokes, he has ZERO ability to do this at home and will keep going and going and going. I know violence isn't the answer but it's really bloody tempting sometimes.

He has this one joke that he's done for years. Actual years. If I'm telling him something serious or upsetting or important, he will always answer, 'Would anal help?' and then laugh at himself, every time. Even though I know it's coming, it makes me want to murder him – because sometimes you just need an actual answer to a question, you know? Also, I have ulcerative colitis, so no, there is quite literally no situation where anal would help, thanks.

Other than his pathological need to make people laugh whether they want to or not, Rob also has Hansel and Gretel syndrome. We laugh about it but I could also quite cheerfully beat him about the head with the next cupboard door he leaves open. I can chart his course around the house and tell you what he's eaten, what he's done and where he's been because Every. Single. Thing will still be out or open. He'd make an excellent victim in *Midsomer Murders* because he'd leave such a detailed set of clues behind. That's also partly why I never worry about him having a sneaky affair, because there's absolutely no way on this earth he'd be able to cover his tracks.

Gemma, Brackley: What's the worst thing Rob has done as a parent?

Taught our four- and six-year-old to say 'piss' and think it's funny. And it is kind of funny, but we had a play date the other day with a beautifully behaved friend of our six-year-old and I was listening to them in horror as our four-year-old proudly explained that they're allowed one rude word a day and theirs was 'piss' – and look! She could spell it as well! So that's probably the last time that child comes to our house, once she goes home and shows off the new vocabulary she learnt at Casa Beckett.

Andy, London: If you weren't with Rob, which celebrity parent would you want to be with instead?

Katherine Ryan without a moment's hesitation. The woman is incredible. She utterly owns, without shame, her life, the way she wants to live it and the way she chooses to raise her children. In my head, she spends her day dressed in ostrich feather pyjamas, being brought champagne by the pool boy while her children ride their golden ponies around the garden swimming pool, and while this (probably) isn't true, I would definitely like some of that parenting action. I try to embrace Katherine's 'fuck it' mentality every time I think I'm being ridiculous or doing something that might be seen as a bit OTT because, honestly, why not enjoy life and your kids where you can? Whoever said, 'Oh no, your child's had too much fun, everything is ruined now'? There's plenty of time for life to be serious and boring; embrace being able to do fun things while they're little enough that they actually want to do them with you and think you're the coolest person in the world. Also, she's fit.

Davina: Who were your teenage heart-throbs and is Rob anything like them?

My teen heartthrobs were Peter Andre and Rupert Grint, neither of which Rob's 'fame' has ever got me close to, sadly, so this marriage has been entirely a waste of time. But looking at the three of them, I realise I could totally go on *Love Island* and say in all honesty that I don't have a 'type'. My other top imaginary boyfriend of the moment is Jack Grealish, which needs zero explanation. All salute our himbo king.

Elizabeth, Whitley Bay: **As a mother it can be hard to maintain your identity, even more so with a famous partner and his challenging working patterns. What do you do to make sure you keep your identity?**

Well, someone's trying to provoke a breakdown for their own entertainment, aren't they?! I don't know really, it's definitely something I've struggled with, especially since I stopped working, as that was a big part of my life. For a (very) brief period of our relationship when I'd just qualified as a teacher and Rob had given up his glamorous admin job to try to do comedy full-time, I was paying our rent and funding our holidays etc., so whenever I feel bad that I don't really contribute financially, I remember that first year or so and the fact he would have starved without me. I was a secondary school history teacher and I loved it, but between a few health things, having the girls and Rob's work schedule it became logistically really difficult. I try to keep the teacher in me alive though by sporadically telling off groups of youths in the street and forcing the girls to listen to the *Six* soundtrack while I interject 'interesting facts' about the Tudors. It really adds to a day out when your four-year-old screeches at the top of her lungs, 'He doesn't want to bang you, somebody hang you,' as you walk past Hever Castle, the home of Anne Boleyn. Incidentally, Hever Castle is a great day out, brilliant playground.

Julia: **Your husband is away a lot on tour. My husband is due to go away with the military soon and I am dreading solo parenting a sassy toddler. Do you have any advice on how to explain it to her, or tips to help pass the time?**

Solo parenting is hard and I have so much respect for people that do it full-time. Firstly, accept any and all help you're offered – there are no prizes for doing everything yourself if you don't have to. If you don't have family or friends nearby who can help you then is there anywhere nearby where you could drop them for an hour or so, especially if they're not in pre-school or nursery yet? Before the girls started pre-school and Rob was away, I joined the gym near our house almost solely so I could use their crèche. I was convinced I was going to transform into one of those terminator gym mums that you see bouncing around in coordinated Lycra making everyone else feel bad. In reality, I swiftly abandoned any pretence at even going to a class and I'd book the girls into the crèche for an hour just so I could shower and get myself dressed for the day without worrying that someone was going to scale the stair gate and splat themselves into the hallway. Then, once I was presentable, I'd have a blissfully quiet cup of hot coffee by myself in the cafe. I always felt really naughty using the crèche to basically get ready for the day instead of exercising but that illicit hour saved my sanity some weeks.

It's always been very much feast or famine for me with Rob being at home. Weirdly, it can sometimes feel just as hard going from no help to loads of help, especially if it's been a while and we've got into a rhythm – sometimes Rob coming home throws that all sideways. I find it much easier to solo parent if

I'm in a routine and I know what's happening each day. Find a rhythm that works for you when you're at home alone and don't feel bad if you're doing less/more than other people as they aren't parenting in your situation, so something's got to give. I know this isn't for everyone but I found looking after the girls much easier and bizarrely less stressful when we were out of the house. It can feel overwhelming starting a day alone with a toddler, or baby, or both, and trying to work out how you're going to make it through until bedtime without all sitting in a corner and having a little cry. I went full nerd and made myself a spreadsheet of every baby group, toddler class, free playgroup, soft play and so on in the area so I knew every day where I could escape the house to.

I'm going to directly contradict myself now, but on the flip side of this, don't overbook yourself or feel bad if you cancel something. I preferred the pay-weekly ad hoc classes/groups rather than the ones where you do a trial and then sign your life away as if it all went horribly wrong that morning and we were all still in our PJs with Weetabix up the walls at 11am then I didn't beat myself up for missing something. When you are solo parenting, whether that is full-time solo or in chunks, then do whatever you need to do to get yourself from A to B with your sanity intact. Toddlers won't remember if they watched 24 straight hours of *Bluey* once in a while. And lastly, remember that parenting is 24/7, so if your partner is coming home after work, then yes, they can be tired but no one is as tired as you. And that is a hill I am prepared to die on.

Stuart, Edinburgh: What is a big beef that you have with your husband (whether he's aware of it or not)?

Rob when he is drunk is an absolute liability. It doesn't happen that much to be fair to him, but when he goes, he absolutely goes and trying to reason with him is like shouting into a storm – utterly useless. I know every wife says this but I honestly don't care what he does or where he goes when he's out. I trust him and he's not a child. So as far as I'm concerned, crack on, drink away, my love, down as many pints as you want, I don't care. What I absolutely don't want to be doing is to be dealing with the consequences of his actions later on. Like during the Euros where Rob's pizza takeaway arrived at the door a full 45 minutes before he did. The doorbell woke the girls up and I had to take delivery of this pizza in the small hours of the morning half asleep in my jimjams. Or on holiday when he went for a 'few drinks' with his new holiday pals to the bar next to the hotel and stayed out till 3am and tried to claim he was not hung-over, just 'very tired' the next day so could I please take the girls to the water park by myself instead of as a family? Or when he insisted repeatedly the only reason he had been out all night and drunk 14 pints on the first day the pubs reopened after lockdown was that he couldn't tell the time on an analogue watch. I don't care that you apparently cannot tell the time, what I care about is you are telling me that at 1.30am when I AM ASLEEP. I wouldn't mind but he's standing by that lie for the last two years and he's still wearing the same watch that is, apparently, incomprehensible to him.

Jasmine, Kent: **How did you find getting used to Rob being online and on TV?**

I met Rob before he had done his first comedy gig, when we were both working for a corporate events company doing admin, so I've seen the progression all the way through, but I still don't think you get used to it, and it's shifted again since we've had the girls. For the most part, it doesn't bother me really as it's been a slow evolution. It has been really interesting watching the girls become aware that people are interested in Rob, though, and them starting to ask questions about why people want to talk to Daddy. They're pretty unfazed for the most part but they definitely get quite protective of him when we are all out together. Because he is away working for chunks of time sometimes, I think they are not very keen on sharing him when he is back and we are out as a family. I don't mind as it comes with the territory and if people weren't interested then Rob wouldn't have a career and I'd be back trying to convince teenagers that a motte-and-bailey castle is actually really cool. Though it does depend on the situation. I don't think there's a parent in the land that wants to stop for a photo when you're on hour seven of Legoland in August summer holidays, with two cross, hungry, overexcited children having a catfight in a double buggy, while the quite frankly demented 'Lego Friends' perform their hourly show at a volume that's both unnecessary and borderline demonic.

Myles, Sarah and baby Sophie: **When you heard that Rob was going to be doing a podcast about parenting, what were your first thoughts?**

That it was an absolutely shameless ploy to get out of parenting during lockdown and that they were quite possibly going to accidentally unleash a Dadsnet-type movement of angry men shouting into the void about the audacity of having to look after their own children. I should have had more faith really as they've created something that I think a lot of people identify with, probably because they've both been so honest with the trials of parenting. Somewhat irritatingly, because it's successful I've now lost any leg I had to stand on while screeching down the garden for Rob to come and help with bedtime while he's recording. Thinking about it now, the times Rob and Josh choose to record sometimes seem a little too convenient... Maybe I should start checking with Rose that Josh is actually recording and Rob isn't just squirrelling himself in his office building Lego.

Helen: **Do you ever listen back to earlier podcasts to remind yourself of earlier parenting struggles?**

I haven't re-listened to any of the earlier ones but I do listen to them weekly just as a kind of one-woman misinformation fact-checking service, as Rob is excellent at taking a seed of truth and growing it into a full-scale forest in the retelling, and it's normally me he's throwing under the bus.

Mike, Loughborough: **Which celebrity guest on the show have you felt you have most in common with when it comes to parenting and why?**

Tom Parry was brilliant – I really identified with the mania of those first few newborn months. Tom's absolute conviction that it was actually going brilliantly and that their plan to just stay awake for 24 hours and trade off periodically was a really good one rather than utter madness, was like looking in a mirror. Rob and I had a few weeks, maybe months, when our oldest was first born that it genuinely seemed easier for one of us to be in the living room with her all night instead of trying to get her to sleep. We'd stay awake for slightly longer than was humanly possible and then when we were about to implode you'd wake the other person up and switch. She was born just before Christmas and I was in the living room with her one night and I didn't realise how long I'd been awake in there until Rob came in as the sun was coming up to see if I was okay and I'd somehow managed to eat my way through both levels of one of those enormous Christmas biscuit tins and watched most of the *Dr Zhivago* remake series on TV, which I've still got no real memory of watching. I'm 99 per cent sure it's about a war and that I fancied James Norton, but that's as much as I can remember from the fog of that period.

Craig and Shirley, Northumberland: What is the biggest lie/exaggeration that Rob and Josh have said on the podcast to make themselves sound better?

I think Rob makes me sound much more uptight than I am about parenting. He makes out like he's some kind of easy breezy super-chilled cool dad about town while I mither in the background. Honestly, though, if I wasn't there mithering about the stuff that Rob thinks 'doesn't really matter' then it would be chaos. There's not a job in the world that Rob couldn't spin a successful PR campaign to abandon if it suited him. I don't think I could ever bring myself to do it but it would be an 'interesting' experiment to go away for a week or so without doing any prep for him at all just to see what happened. Even when I went into hospital for a while unexpectedly I was still issuing instructions from the ward about who needed to wear what uniform on which day and how to use the washing machine.

Alison: Do you actually find your husband funny?

It depends on how many times he's asked 'if anal would help' that day.

Juliette: How quiet is the house when Rob is away?

The house is never that quiet as the girls can make an impressive amount of noise for two small people – they are Rob's children after all – but while it's not quiet it is at least tidy. That's one of the unexpected perks of having a husband who works away a lot – sure, I do a lot of solo parenting but there's a particular joy in tidying the house once the girls have gone to bed and knowing when I come down in the morning that it will still be tidy, instead of finding a trail of clothes, plates, open cupboards and ripped-open parcels. That's something else that annoys me, actually – when Rob opens a parcel he rips it open like a caveman, which is fine unless you want to return anything and then I'm there trying to tape the box back together like I'm on *Art Attack*.

Julie: **How annoying is it when you're irritated with your husband and you turn on the Sky Plus box and see his face on the home screen?**

Maddening. Normally because he's doing something fun on these TV shows and it's really hard to remember that it's 'work' when he's been off being stupid with Romesh. I'm not a big enough person not to get a very childish level of satisfaction when he's at least being made to do something awful or humiliating – it feels like a bit of TV-sanctioned balance has been restored when he's made to get a colonic on telly and bits of his own poo are floating past him in a little hosepipe.

Helen: **If you could give yourself (pre-children) a piece of parenting advice, what would it be?**

To not worry as much. I drove myself absolutely loopy with our first about breastfeeding. I was absolutely single-minded about her only getting breast milk and that being the best thing, even in the face of all evidence to the contrary. She couldn't latch properly so I was expressing instead, which would have been fine apart from I also, for whatever reason, wasn't brilliant at expressing either. So I was expressing every few hours, day and night, for months on end and it was fucking madness that not a single midwife or health visitor stepped in and said it would be okay to just give her a bottle. Instead, everyone in our house was tired, hungry and cross for about four solid months. I'd be so embarrassed when we were out and the other NCT mums were breastfeeding at whatever ridiculous baby group we were at that day. But it was so unnecessary as no one else gave a single monkey's about what I was doing other than me.

That's a quite specific bit of advice about feeding but you can broaden that out to having your ideas of how you want to do things but also not worrying if it doesn't work. Suddenly having a baby to look after is such a stressful situation; you start physically exhausted from pregnancy and labour and then you're meant to just take this screaming potato baby home and magically know how to look after it, when in any other situation, if your body had gone through that you'd be kept in hospital to recuperate for a week or so and then maybe sent to a spa for good measure. There's no one handing out medals for giving birth without pain relief or having a breakdown over breastfeeding, so more power to you if you manage it but also power to the people who make whatever decision is right for them without going into a futile guilt spiral of doom.

Sophie, Wales: What would be your top five parenting tips?

1. In the words of RuPaul, 'Unless they paying your bills, pay them bitches no mind.' There's literally more parenting advice and rules and methods than any one

person could ever follow in a lifetime, so try your best to work out what's right for you and your family without feeling guilty. I have failed at this massively, so it's easier said than done, I know.

2. Pick your battles – toddlers are savage and they aren't as tired as you. They have more stamina to ride out a stand-off, so pick which battles you want to fight judiciously. Save the big guns for the stuff you really care about and if you can't win then don't pick the fight.

3. Always have emergency stickers in your bag – I get these packs of A5 sheets from Amazon which are animal faces with lots of eyes/ears/accessories to create your own face and they're brilliant. And people are always weirdly impressed with your parenting skills if you can pull out stickers at any given opportunity.

4. Something I learnt when I was teaching and they sent me on a course for behaviour management (speaks volumes about my teaching, doesn't it?!) was the pre-emptive thank you. So if I want the girls to do something I say, 'I need you to put your shoes on by the time we get to one, thank you very much. In, THREE, thank you for your good listening, TWO, brilliant work, let's go, excellent doing, and ONE, your shoes should be on now, and finished, thank you for your good listening and good doing.' It doesn't always work but interjecting the countdown with assumptions of compliance, thank yous and reminders of what they should be doing seems to help them remember what I'm actually asking them to do and that it isn't an option to not do it because I'm assuming they're already doing it and thanking them.

I've made that sound like I can Jedi mind trick them into doing whatever I say in a lovely calm manner, but equally, I can often be heard screaming like a banshee for them to PLEASE PUT THEIR SHOES ON RIGHT NOW AS I AM LEAVING RIGHT NOW I BEG OF YOU PUT ON YOUR SHOES NO THEY AREN'T YOUR SHOES, THESE ARE YOUR SHOES, NO THAT'S THE WRONG FEET, WHERE ARE YOU GOING?, NO YOU CAN'T GET CHANGED WE'RE LATE FOR SCHOOL several times a week. But we can all dream, right?

5. And lastly, no matter how much it might seem like it sometimes, your partner is not the enemy. Children are masters of the divide and conquer so remember you're one team and however much you might want to throttle your partner, don't let the children sense any weakness between you as they'll be on that before you know it. Parenting is like guerrilla warfare; keep your wits about you and when it seems suspiciously calm that's when to brace yourself.

Mike, Loughborough: What is your best memory as a family so far?

We went to Disney this year and I think it was one of the best times we've ever had as a family. Sure, I was in bed with a medicinal wine by about 9.30pm most nights, but it was so worth it. The girls were young enough at four and six to really be excited about the 'magic' but also old enough to go on the rides and not need a full baby bag of essentials. It's so liberating being able to go away now and not have to take baby food, or special cups they can drink out of, or flasks of boiled water. You don't realise until it stops how much extra thinking you're doing just to get out of the house.

Between Rob's workload and all the Covid restrictions of the past few years, it felt like this holiday had been so long coming and we were all so excited about it, and it was one of those rare-ish times when (apart from an absolutely ideal 4am flight cancellation) nothing disappointed. It was everything I needed it to be, just really solid uninterrupted family time making memories.

Kayla, Cheltenham: What has been Rob's most ridiculous purchase?

Thinking about it, this is another of my 'beefs' with Rob – some of the ludicrous stuff he turns up with when he's been shopping unaccompanied by a responsible adult. The amount of ridiculous Lego sets we've got in the house is farcical at this point – there's just Lego everywhere! He wanted to put shelving units in the living room and make a display case of sorts but I just cannot bring myself to sanction a whole room of Lego. It'd be like living in a weird Lego museum. Imagine trying to watch *Love Island* around a Batmobile display case? So I've drawn a decorative line in the sand. He might need a Lego shed or something he can display everything in. That or a divorce.

Rachel, Merseyside: What was Rob like when you went into labour? My husband was great but I honestly think he found the whole thing more traumatic than me – he didn't even realise something was weird when my son was born still in his sac until the midwife pointed it out.

My first labour was a bit chaotic as we were sent back home to wait the first time we went into hospital and then it escalated quite quickly. The trainee midwife kept telling me that my labour wouldn't move very fast and I 'didn't have a frame of reference' for the pain, so I wasn't actually in as much pain as I thought I was so I couldn't have an epidural yet. Which turned out to be utter bollocks and made me so angry. I went from 2cm to 10cm in two hours to make everyone panic out of pure spite. It's a bit of a delirious blur to be honest as I'd been throwing up from the pain all day, so in between contractions I was a bit spaced out. Rob was brilliant during labour even though he felt a bit helpless. He liked having a job to do, so he hunted down a can of cold, full-sugar Coca-Cola and to this day, it's still one of the best things I've ever drunk.

My second labour was much calmer because I was so much firmer with what I needed. When I say firmer, I was an absolute screaming banshee in that first assessment room with a lovely midwife who was doing her absolute best. I would not listen to a single thing I was being asked. I think I kind of screeched on repeat: 'I went two to ten in two hours last time; I want an epidural. NO, I do not want to look at the birth centre, I want an epidural. NO, I'm not going home to wait, I want an epidural. I'll sit outside the doors until you give me an epidural.' I think they could sense an impending panic attack from this hysterical pregnant lady in front of them and admitted me straight away and honestly, when the epidural hit, it was absolute magic. The rest of that labour was lovely. I had a nap, read my magazine. Rob went to the M&S garage next to the hospital and, for some inexplicable reason, bought a Ferrero Rocher tower complete with 72 Ferrero Rochers. He then started to eat his sandwich next to me after the midwife had told me I couldn't eat now the epidural was in and he got such a withering look from both of us as he cracked the packet open that he went to eat it in the toilet by himself. We've still got that Ferrero Rocher tower and it comes out every Christmas.

Mike, Loughborough: **What would be the biggest difference if you and Rose were doing a podcast instead of Rob and Josh?**

I think it would be more about the trials and tribulations of managing Josh and Rob parenting the kids rather than just the kids!

Sleep

'The only people who should be up at 4am are people who have booked a cheap flight and people coming back from illegal raves.'

Rob: Sleep is the biggest problem facing all parents and anyone in the world that has to deal with sleep-deprived parents. Lack of sleep is crippling, you literally cannot function. Having children is basically the same as having jet lag for at least four years non-stop. For the non-parents reading this, jet lag is the closest thing to having children. With jet lag all you think about is, when can I sleep? When is it okay to sleep? If I sit down there on my own, I'm so jet-lagged I will fall asleep. But I can't do that as it will be dangerous because I'm looking after a child/I'm a bus driver (delete as appropriate).

Josh: I think the happiest Rob has ever been was the first three months of my son's life, when he was completely incapable of sleeping for more than an hour at a time. And Rob was right to enjoy it. If we are honest, that is the greatest joy of parenting: finding someone who has it worse than you. Yes, Rob got woken up every morning at 6am by two children who had inherited his trademark slightly intense energy, but at least he wasn't me, a man who considered 90 minutes without a wake-up as relaxing as two weeks in Puglia. Of all the sleep tips I can give you, top of the list is to find a friend whose children sleep worse than yours – even at your lowest ebb it will bring you huge consolation (Hello, Tom Craine!).

Now I have come through those dark, sleepless nights of summer 2021, I almost look back on it as an amusing chapter in my life. Blimey, remember that summer when I used to walk round a park on three hours' sleep at 6am just to get out of the house and see other humans – what was I like? But in reality I know that it didn't feel amusingly quirky at the time and I know this because for a week or so during this period I wrote a diary in my phone of what I was going through to read out on the podcast. I then never read it out as I felt it sounded too bleak and, if I'm honest, like I was having a breakdown. And yes, I am aware that starting to write a diary for the first time in your life while looking after a newborn and getting three hours' sleep a night is like deciding to do an Open University degree while also being on trial for murder. But I think, from reading it, I wasn't in a great place in terms of decision-making. So, as an exclusive to this book (mainly as no one else would ever think of publishing it), let's all settle down for some words from the phone notes of Josh Widdicombe 2021 (apologies in advance for the swearing).

Saturday, 19 June 2021

Sleep is 96 per cent of the battle in parenting. There are other things that can be tough but nothing compares to the grim, life-dominating existence of having a child that doesn't sleep. I don't care if your child is a fussy eater, it doesn't compare –

once you have thrown the sweet potato in the bin and given her a Fab, quite frankly it won't affect your life. It doesn't take over your mind throughout the day or make you dread something as unavoidable as the sun going down. A baby that can't sleep does that. Today I sat and just stared for ten minutes before I could come up with the effort to put on my second sock, and that doesn't happen to someone because their child has decided they will only eat red apples. For the whole day everything is tough, every moment an effort. I was wrong – sleep is 99 per cent of the battle.

Sunday, 20 June 2021

He screamed for no reason from 6pm to 9pm last night. That is the same running time as *The Godfather*. My daughter had colic and I fear he does as well. Colic is a posh word for your baby screaming in your face for no reason for hours and hours every evening and no one being able to explain why it is happening. And it is less fun than that sounds.

I didn't used to think about sleep, it was never something I considered as a luxury. I presumed it would always be part of life like showering or *Pointless*, but then suddenly it was gone. Like showering. I never thought that one day I would go to bed nervous, panicked that I was heading towards disaster. I'd make a joke about sex here but I'm too tired to work it out.

Monday, 21 June 2021

Just remembered a book I read where it said to get a baby to sleep, all you need to do is stroke their nose and I laughed out loud.

Tuesday, 22 June 2021

I described my son screaming for three hours to a parent today and they said, 'Maybe he is just a fussy baby.' Has the word fussy completely changed its meaning? For the first 38 years of my life, fussy meant someone that didn't like to have raisins in their muesli. Since having a child, this has suddenly come to mean someone screaming and screaming and screaming. He's not fussy, he's not turning down milk because it is a little too warm coming out of the boob. He's crying actual tears and shitting on my hand. Were someone to do that when sitting next to you in a restaurant, you wouldn't call them fussy, you would call the police. Or at the very least the maître d'.

Wednesday, 23 June 2021

Seriously, why did we decide to have a baby a month before Euro 2020? This is insane. I just spent an evening with the curtains closed in our room, in the pitch-fucking-black as France got knocked out of the fucking tournament. Meanwhile I'm trying desperately to get him to sleep, his eyes slowly closing. (Why do babies close their eyes a tiny bit at a time depending on how close they are to sleep? Like a progress update on a file you are downloading.) I tried to watch the game silently on my phone, but it was ruined by people texting me about the game, giving away what was about to happen as they were ahead of me because they weren't watching on a fucking phone!!! 'What a goal!' they would say and I would know in two minutes there would be a goal. And by that point my son would be awake again anyway, because even if he does go to sleep, he will

100 per cent wake up for the first six attempts at putting him in his fucking cot.

Rob: I can't believe he kept a diary. No wonder he's so tired all the time – he's setting himself his own homework. Now before having children I never drank coffee, I couldn't even stand the smell of it. No matter how busy my life was or how hung-over I was or how jet-lagged I was, I had never drunk it. I used to present the spin-off show to *I'm A Celebrity... Get Me Out of Here!*, which had the snappy and catchy title of *I'm A Celebrity... Get Me Out Of Here Now!* That show was filmed in Australia, which is a place where jet lag is as extreme as it gets. The jet lag cannot get any worse than Australia, because if you fly to Australia and keep on going, the jet lag hits a tipping point then starts to get better as you head back home, until you're back on the same time zone. It's a benefit of the earth being a sphere. Apologies to any flat-earthers reading this. I haven't woken up yet. I'm still one of the sheep being spoon-fed lies by 'the system'. Totally understand if you stop reading the book. That's your call. With your new-found free time can I suggest you get in a boat and sail west from Southampton for as long as you can and when you end up back in Southampton in about a year's time, I expect a full written apology. Anyway, this show I presented (*IACGMOOHN*) was filmed and broadcast live at 8am in Oz so it was on at 10pm UK time. Essentially I was on nights in Australia working from 11pm to 9am and severely jet-lagged. I was so tired, jet-lagged and confused when I arrived in Australia that I pissed myself. But even then I didn't think to have a coffee. Not until I had children did I become so weak and exhausted that I got tempted into the seductive and addictive world of the coffee bean.

I am now a complete slut for coffee. I sometimes get excited to go to sleep because I know I can have my first coffee of the day soon. How pathetic is that? I lay there thinking, *Rob, you are such a loser. Thirty years you survived with no coffee and now you're completely addicted because of two little, beautiful blonde shits.*

Now I know what you're thinking. Tell us about the time you pissed yourself in Australia. Not a problem, reader. Here it comes. I was asleep in my pants. Well, I was asleep in my bed wearing my pants. I wasn't curled up in a massive pair of pants. I woke up in a tired, discombobulated, jet-lagged haze and went to the toilet. I stood in front of the toilet and started to urinate. However I was so tired I forgot to remove my penis from my pants. So I stood in front of a toilet and pissed myself. Standing there in a puddle of my own piss, alone on the other side of the world on the eve of my first big TV gig. Show business is so glamorous – from goose shit to human piss in just a few months. The weird thing is I don't even really like the smell or taste of coffee – I just like the way it makes me feel.

Josh: While it may not seem that I dealt with things brilliantly when my son wouldn't sleep, I did have a number of coping mechanisms. The first of these was to repeatedly utter that most simple of parenting mantras: 'everything's a phase'. Don't worry how bad it is because this is just a moment, children change and one day it will not be like this. That's right, wish your life away. Everything. Is. A. Phase. This didn't offer much comfort, because to be frank, the knowledge that one day in the far distant future I will get to sleep is not hugely helpful when at this exact moment it is 2.46am, I've been up since 12.31am and my older child will be waking up at 6am. At that moment I quite frankly couldn't care less that I will be able to catch up on some sleep in 2026.

We all have our own ways of coping. I have a friend whose two-year-old son would only go to sleep if they had physical contact. A couple of nights ago he texted me to say that in an attempt to get his son to sleep he was lying next to his bed holding his hand and that he had been there for two and a half hours (as I say, find friends that have it worse than you). Scared to look at his phone too much and distract his son, my friend was left with nothing but his own thoughts, spending the time counting to 100 again and again in an attempt to calm himself down. It was – as he described with huge understatement – a situation that was 'unsustainable in the long run'. How did my friend get through this without screaming, 'I just want my life back!' or, worse, starting a podcast to complain about it? He told me that when he was at his lowest he would think about his five-year-old daughter: 'I just say to myself that there is no one in the world I like talking to more than her and one day my son will also be that age.' It's a great tip, unless it is your first child that isn't sleeping, in which case you will have nothing to hold on to. And what's worse, you are probably going to decide to go through all this again.

One of the strangest ways I found of coping was to convince myself that I was actually okay with starting the day at 5am. When my son was doing his early wake-ups, the Tokyo Olympics was on TV, and I would justify that it was fine to take him downstairs, watching Britain claim a silver in the BMX would be inspiring for him in the long run. But then the Olympics ended and I was stuck with a child that woke up at 5am. For some reason, I stuck to my story and claimed that I was fine with 5ams. Who wouldn't want to turn on the radio to find the breakfast show hasn't even started yet; that your wake-up has been deemed by BBC 6 Music to be before anyone in their right minds would be up? Who wouldn't want to WhatsApp people and then wait three hours for a reply because they hadn't got up yet? (Small tip if you are up early: check the WhatsApp profile of parents with children that sleep worse than yours and enjoy the words 'last seen today at 3.34am'. Imagining what they were up to at that point can really get you through a morning.)

And then just when I had justified the 5am starts to myself, it got much, much worse. The clocks went back. The man who came up with the idea of the clocks changing should be tried for war crimes at The Hague. Suddenly a child that wakes up at 6am is a child that wakes up at 5am. And, more importantly for me, a child that wakes up at 5am is a child that wakes up at 4am. FOUR AM! The only people who should be up at 4am are people who have booked a cheap flight and people coming back from illegal raves. To be honest it isn't even the first bit after 4am that is the problem. It's actually okay when you are chilling out at 4.45am, absolutely buzzing from your third tea of the day. It is when you get to 8am and it feels like early afternoon. You've been up four hours, it still isn't even time for *Frasier* and you are eating lunch. That is why people put on weight after having a kid: their day now has six mealtimes.

Perhaps the worst bit about the clocks changing is the glee of people without kids. 'What are you going to do with your extra hour?' they will ask you, looking at you with worry as you answer 'Stare into the abyss.' 'Oh, right, well I think I may lie in, or maybe I'll do a HIIT class,' they will reply. Meanwhile I am preparing for a life of going to bed at 8pm just to get my eight hours. 8pm! No one should be brushing their teeth during *The One Show*. And yes, I know at another point in the year the clocks readjust back (or is it forwards, I never know) but that never seems to help either as somehow that still messes up their sleep. For parents, the clocks are somehow always changing in the wrong direction.

Rob: Wow, by accident I think Josh might have written a really profound statement about parenting. 'For parents, the clocks are somehow always changing in the wrong direction.' Jesus Christ, he's just made me think about dying for 20 minutes. Now when you're not worrying about your own mortality/lack of sleep, you are working out how to get your kids to sleep and then keep them asleep. I used to drive my kids around in my car at night to get them to sleep. It always worked. But the problem is trying to move them from the car up the stairs and into their cot without waking them. (Hey, guys, just want to check my privilege here. Yes, I do have an upstairs. I don't want to offend any bungalow owners.) The movement of a sleeping child from a car to a bed should be an Olympic sport. It's so difficult, you need to be strong but gentle and also really good with angles. A combination of Eddie Hall, Mother Teresa and Pythagoras. It's like a maths project there's so many gaps and spaces you need to manoeuvre yourself and your sleeping child through. On top of this you are doing these movements in complete darkness and in complete silence in order to keep the child asleep. If you bash your elbow on a door frame you cannot make a sound, you are only allowed to open your mouth and scream with pain internally. The scream swallower, I like to call it.

Josh: And so we arrived at sleep training, a phrase which conjures up images of your child in a locked room crying while outside a woman who looks like Miss Trunchbull screws another bolt on the door and shouts: 'It's good for you in the long run.' And I have to be honest, at our lowest ebb we wouldn't have rejected that scenario out of hand (NB we would, just in case social services are reading). The first thing our sleep trainer told us was that our main mistake was when we repeatedly got our son up to watch the Olympics at 5am. Which MAY have taught him that was the time the day started. What we're saying here is the blame firmly lay with ~~the Olympics~~ me.

To solve this problem we were told that when he woke up, we had to go in and resettle him (rub his back in the vain hope of calming him down) and then leave. And then when he started crying again go back in and resettle and leave. And go back in. And leave. And go back in... etc. until 6am. In theory easy, in practice the longest two hours of your life. I'm not saying at points it felt like it wasn't working, but at one stage I was going in and resettling him once every 30 to 45 seconds – that's around 90 resettles before 6am. Desperate for something to get me through, I tried to use these gaps to make a cup of tea. Run downstairs, kettle on. Run upstairs, resettle. Run downstairs, teabag in mug. Run upstairs, resettle. Run downstairs, pour hot water in mug. Run upstairs, resettle. Run downstairs, teabag out. Run upstairs, resettle. Run downstairs, milk in. Run upstairs, resettle. Run downstairs, milk back in fridge. Run upstairs spilling tea in panic, resettle. It's always good to get your 10,000 steps in before 6am – that way you can sit on the sofa and stare into the distance for the next 14 hours.

We did this for a week. It was – and I need to be clear about this – not a laugh. But then it started to work, his desperate need to watch live taekwondo at five in the morning was leaving him. The gaps got bigger between resettles and before I knew it, I could make a cup of tea in one go (maybe two goes). And eventually, after about three weeks, we were left with a baby that slept until 6am. The joy we felt only tempered by the regret that we hadn't thought to do this three months ago. That and the ultimate fear that we knew these 6am wake-ups wouldn't last. Worryingly, everything is a phase.

Rob: My kids are currently six and four and they sleep pretty well now but get up early. Which I hope is a phase. It's obviously a million times better than when they were newborns, but I'm still always tired. I keep thinking it will get better when they get older but I don't think it will. I've worked out that by the time they are old enough for you to sleep properly, they are old enough to go to the pub. So then they no longer wake you up early in the morning. What they do instead is keep you up to 3am waiting for them to come home. Basically, what I'm saying is, if you have kids, you're completely fucked and you will never sleep properly again until you're dead.

P*ss, Sh*t and S*ck

'So I did what any good parent would do –
I used my finger to help roll the rock-hard ball
of poo out of her.'

As you will be able to tell from the title, this chapter is almost exclusively about the liquids that come out of your child, so if you are of a squeamish disposition then we would advise skipping on to us grumbling about feeding in the next chapter.

Rob: I'll never forget it. My first-born daughter was six months old. I was 30 years of age and we were in the beautiful seaside town of Calella in northern Spain. The weather was too warm for her and we were only getting tiny amounts of milk down her. She was also refusing to drink water. We weren't too worried as she was bright-eyed and energetic, so we concluded that she was getting enough liquid but not loads of the stuff. The issue was the lack of number twos. We were on day six of a seven-day holiday and she had still not done a poo.

On the morning of the sixth day, she was in her buggy squirming and wriggling with the brightest red face I have ever seen. It was 28 degrees but her face looked like it was on a mini break to Dubai in July. Her face was so red it looked like she was about to explode. I took her to the baby change room, stripped her completely naked and fanned her to try and cool her down. She was red-hot to the touch. I then watched her attempt to push out a rock-hard, perfectly round ball of shit. It looked like an actual brown golf ball was being evacuated from her body. This went on for about 20 minutes – I knew I had to intervene. She had done most of the work but she couldn't get it over the line. Like an exhausted London Marathon runner falling to their knees on the Mall just in front of Buckingham Palace. One hundred metres from glory. So I did what any good parent would do – I used my finger to help roll the rock-hard ball of poo out of her.

That's something you have to accept and emotionally process as a parent. You will have human shit on your hands on multiple occasions. As this solid sphere of shit was finally prised from my darling baby's bottom, my daughter instantly went back to her normal skin tone. Like Princess Fiona in *Shrek* turning from ogre to human. She smiled the brightest of smiles and laughed and giggled and kicked her legs in joy. It was a living hell and a magical moment all at the same time. We had gone on a journey together – my helpless child needed me and I was there to help. She was beside herself with relief and glee, it felt so special. But I couldn't really surrender to the moment and experience it as I still had shit all over my hands. That's what parenting is: moments of unparalleled joy interrupted by human shit and panic.

Josh: I actually quite like doing the nappy change. Not in some earth mother way. I'm not about to tell you that I love my children so much that I actually consider their faeces to be part of them and consequently I see smelling their nappy as a further bonding opportunity. No, I simply mean that cleaning shit off a child isn't nearly as bad as I thought it would be. In fact, it is one of the few bits of being a dad that I can confidently say I nail every time. Baby on mat, nappy off, wet wipes out, wipe up shit, fold wipes into nappy, apply overly expensive ointment that Rose bought and I'm not sure does anything, new nappy on, old nappy in bin, Babygro on. Done, clinical. It's like watching the SAS take out a terrorist. Or at least change a terrorist's nappy.

I am as surprised as anyone that I am good at this as I have always had an unreasonably sensitive gag reflex. On a bad day even brushing my teeth can lead to me retching in the sink like an ex-*EastEnders* actor doing a bush tucker trial (a worrying sign for my inevitable career downturn). Anything can make me retch: cat food, the thought of a slug, drinking eight pints of lager – really innocent things. This has its own issues in that I never realise when something is actually wrong. One Edinburgh Festival I found myself retching in the shower every morning and just put it down to my usual gag reflex issues, only to find out two weeks into my stay that in fact there was a gas leak in my bedroom. I had essentially been sleeping in a gas canister for a fortnight. When the man came to fix it I said, 'So could I have died?' and he replied, 'No, it's fine,' adding wistfully, 'gone are the days you could kill yourself in a gas oven.' Which was reassuring.

But here I am 12 years later, a man who is regularly pissed on and shat on by his own child without coming close to retching. Let's get one thing clear, this is no way to live a life. No one should be okay with being pissed or shat on (except a few celebrities I've heard rumours about paying for such a service). But for some reason when I hold my son's legs back to change his nappy and shit fires out of him like a nightmarish super soaker, I don't see this as the lowest point of my life. I find myself saying things like, 'Oh, it's only milk,' overlooking that it clearly isn't only milk because it is an electric brown colour previously only seen in the patterns of 1970s wallpaper. When did I start caring about shit based on the diet of the person who was producing it? 'No, don't worry, shit anywhere you like; you're a vegan.'

What Rob doesn't realise is it is much easier with daughters; when it comes to changing a nappy, the vagina is far preferable to the penis. Going from changing my daughter's nappy to my son's was like the time I converted from PC to Apple – suddenly all the shortcuts I knew didn't exist. To get technical for a minute, if my daughter decided to do a piss while I was changing her nappy, that would just go downwards into the nappy or, usually, on to my shoes. With a boy lying on his back, the urine will shoot up into the air with the majestic range of a fountain in a European town square. Were the sun to shine through the window at that moment, you'd get that rainbow effect that happens with a garden sprinkler, but with slightly less temptation to run through it.

And you might think, *Well, how often does your son piss at the exact moment the nappy comes off?* and the answer would be all the time. Get this: apparently there is something about the penis that means when it hits fresh air it makes it piss, like a movement sensor porch light. This means when changing a nappy you have to try and cover the penis at all times, holding a cotton pad on it the moment it sees daylight, like a soldier jumping on a landmine to save his platoon. If changing a nappy was a computer game, the penis would be the end of level boss.

Rob: Josh is absolutely right. It's going to sound like I'm bragging, but my daughters don't have penises so I've not had too much trouble with piss as a parent. That's one of the great things about vaginas – everything is much neater and tidier compared to the loose cannon nature of a human's penis. A little baby penis can piss all over you immediately if you're not quick on the draw with a nappy shield. We had the odd bed-wetting incident at the start but my girls were out of nappies at night quite early and stuck with it.

Josh: The big news early doors as a parent is that babies shit 12 times a day. Which seems excessive – I once did five on a hangover and phoned NHS direct.[2] But 12?! I know there isn't much distance between mouth and nappy but surely they don't need to be knocking out a dozen every 24 hours. It is a statistic that feels like some kind of terrible brag from the worst person on a stag do, the thing they tell you after they have just claimed to have slept with an FHM High Street Honey.

The problem is, 12 shits into eight waking hours just doesn't go. So you find yourself with the greatest moral conundrum of the new parent: what do you do when your baby does a shit in their sleep?

A. Wake them to change their nappy and then struggle to get them back to sleep
B. Let them sleep in their own shit so that you can go back to sleep

Like all first-timers, we initially thought the correct answer was A – you can't let your child sleep in their own shit.

---

2 I was fine.

Then after about one day of parenthood, it started to feel like there was a good argument to be made for answer B. You might think this is bad parenting but you have to understand we had a solid reason why we believed this to be okay, and that reason was: no one needs to know we did this. This is a secret between me, you and the baby – and we know she can't talk. It's the perfect crime. (This was before I had signed this lucrative deal for a tell-all book about my baby's bowel movements.)

But you can't clean shit out of a nappy forever, however much you want to. And so eventually you come to potty training. I'm not going to offer any tips on when to do it, all I will say is I have friends that waited so long that they managed to train their daughter from nappy to toilet in 48 hours. They are either geniuses or negligent parents (I won't name them in case it is the second of these).

Sadly, we didn't take the option to wait until our daughter was doing her GCSEs and so we set out on a slightly longer road from nappy to potty. I would like to start by saying I am no expert on potty training and as evidence to back this up we put the potty in the kitchen. Yes, that's right, a toilet in the kitchen. The kind of detail you would find out about a mad dictator: 'Oh yeah, Colonel Gaddafi had a toilet in his kitchen; people were just too scared to say it was weird.'

Maybe this quite intense potty position is why we had a very different training experience to Rob's life of wall-to-wall, 24/7 shits in his slippers. For while his was a case of feast, ours was far more a case of famine. Our daughter had decided she was too old for nappies but she had also decided that she wasn't that into the potty, and so rather than use either option she was just going to never shit again. If you have ever had stage fright at a urinal because a man with a Millwall tattoo has stood next to you (hypothetically, this has definitely never happened to me), well, she had this for days on end. Food was going into her but it wasn't coming out. Where was it? Was she disposing of it out of her trouser leg at nursery like Steve McQueen in *The Great Escape*?

It was around day three when we began to panic, dreaming of living in the Beckett household and finding a turd in our bed. They didn't know how lucky they were. They weren't spending their days googling 'Can you die from never having a shit again?' Or 'Can you have done all your shits by the age of three?' It turns out parenthood is a story of not knowing what you've got till it's gone, be that a toddler holding your hand, a baby laughing, or it seems, faeces.

If you're looking for a tip on how to get through this then once again I have to say, I have nothing. For after about a week she finally decided this was not a good idea in the long term and there it was, a turd in a potty in the corner of our kitchen. Which in one way was a positive but in another way really put me off my cheese and onion toastie.

Rob: That serves him right for putting 'onion' in a sandwich. I may have avoided being pissed on but I have to say that there's been a lot more vomit in my life than I thought there would be when we first found out Lou was pregnant. Some nights my house resembles a spew-covered bar street in Ayia Napa. You weirdly just get used to cleaning sick up. It gets to the point where you have experienced so many moments of sickness that you can rate them from best to worst.

The best sick I've ever dealt with was the Haribo sick driving back from the airport. My daughter was unwell on the plane, with a temperature. She didn't want any food, she just drank water and ate some/too much Haribo. All was fine until five minutes from home – it's always five minutes from home, isn't it? – when she projectile vomited all over herself, the car seat, the back of the seat in front of her, the footwell and the back of my head. Initially I was panicked and disgusted. Until I touched and smelt the sick – it was literally Haribo-flavoured water. The car actually smelt better after she had been sick. It was like a fruity air freshener had been sprayed in the car. Honestly, if you served me a pint of it I would have thought it was some sort of fruit cordial.

My daughter has been sick on a plate of chips in a restaurant for what felt like no reason whatsoever. She immediately felt better and was laughing about it 20 minutes later as she polished off an ice cream. Once on holiday my daughter was sick all over herself in the car outside of a *supermercado* which led to us walking up and down the aisle with a naked toddler as we attempted to buy her a new outfit in the Spanish version of George at Asda aisle.

Another great sick was on a boat trip in Tenerife when we went out to find a pod of migrating pilot whales at sunset. It was one of the most beautiful evenings with a glorious sunset. As the sky glowed orange as the sun was setting, we came across the whales; it felt like being in a Sir David Attenborough nature documentary. We were in the middle of the ocean totally alone. The boat engine was switched off, we couldn't even see the shoreline. We were floating along with the tide and these real-life whales in complete silence. The only noise we could hear was the wales' blowholes as they came to the surface for a breath of air. It was an unbelievable sound. I felt like I was creating a core memory at the same time with my wife and children. It felt like a true-life version of all those Instagram photos that look fake. It was a genuine moment in time that we would all remember together. And it will be remembered forever by all the Becketts involved but for the wrong reasons.

The silence was broken once again, this time not by the beauty of a whale breathing but by my four-year-old retching. She was seasick, violently seasick. My poorly darling baby hanging over the edge of the boat being sick on top of a whale. Actual sick landed on a whale – the poor whale must have thought it was some sort of hate crime. I couldn't believe it – my first time seeing a whale in real life and my daughter has been sick on it.

We turned back to shore as the whales continued on with their migration. We arrived back as the sun had completely vanished and I said to Lou that we should get her back to the hotel room and into bed as she was unwell. Only to turn round to see her on a climbing frame in a park topless. She had made a full recovery in seconds of being on dry land. We bought her a new dress and tied up her sick-covered hair. (There was no way of washing it in the sea or a bar toilet: damage limitation until we got back to the hotel.) After the park and climbing frame we headed back to the hotel, but as we passed the entertainment clubhouse, my daughters heard 'Agadoo' pumping out of the speakers at the kids' disco and ran in before we could even say, 'No, you've got sick in your hair.' Within one hour we had gone from whale watching to dancing to 'Agadoo' with sick in your hair. Children are relentless and unstoppable, and you've got to respect how hardcore they are.

Feeding

'My daughter has one simple food rule: it must be beige... there she is, night after night, her plate with the colour palette of a pensioner's wardrobe.'

Josh: Before having a child, my understanding was that if you had problems feeding your offspring this could be solved simply by pretending the spoon was an aeroplane. Within minutes of birth, you realise this is just another area of parenthood that isn't as simple as you thought. Suddenly the unique majesty of holding your newborn is replaced with questions. Are they latching on? Are they taking in milk? Are they refusing the milk because they are vegan? Does human milk count as vegan? Why am I asking all these questions?

Rob: We had a nightmare feeding our kids. Breastfeeding was a disaster from the start with our firstborn. She didn't latch on properly and was so small at birth. She weighed 5lbs 11oz! We had a breastfeeding nurse sent from hell at the hospital that basically bullied Lou like she was in Year 7 at school. Lou tried the best she could at a huge cost to her own health and well-being but it just wasn't happening. So we had to move on to formula, and once on formula we found out that the baby was allergic to dairy. 'How do you know if your baby is allergic to dairy?' was asked a lot by people assuming we were snowflake hipsters making up allergies for attention. The quandary 'How do you know if your baby is allergic to dairy?' is quite simply answered in two words: 'Shit everywhere.' Human shit all over the place. Up the back, in the ears, on the face, the windows, the ceiling, the wall. Like a scatological recital of 'Wind the Bobbin Up'. If you google 'Is my baby allergic to dairy?' there's a long list of symptoms: rash, spitting up, belly ache, etc. When in reality it should say, 'If your baby is allergic to dairy you won't be able to read this because your phone screen will be covered in shit.'

We then had to switch to dairy-free formula which stops the mess, however what you do get instead is green-coloured poo. Which the doctor didn't warn us about, which sent us into another frenzied Google search. At the start she didn't want the new dairy-free formula, she kept on spitting it out. So for a whole day our daughter didn't have any milk. We were ravaged with worry and anxiety, and just thinking back to it now makes me all hot and stressed. We were getting so stressed that she would starve.

In the afternoon/early evening I took her for a walk, then sat in the park with her and spent at least an hour trying to get this tiny baby to take the new formula. Eventually she relented, and I like to think I had some special method that cracked the code. But the truth is more likely my daughter was thirsty and hungry and thought, *Fuck it, there's no dairy coming my way. I might as well choke down this weird drink that makes my shit turn green.* She chugged down a 16th of a bottle of milk, and I'm talking a tiny newborn-sized bottle, so basically a dribble of milk. I have never been so happy and elated – it was like

England winning the World Cup. I rang Lou immediately and told her, 'I've done it, Lou. I've only gone and done it. She's had at least 14 millilitres of non-dairy formula.' Lou was beside herself with joy. Such a pathetically small amount of milk, but it was a start. For two exhausted parents covered in shit, that was earth-shatteringly good news.

A lot of comedians remember where they were when they first got asked to be on *Live at the Apollo*. I think I was on a bus – I can't quite place myself. However there will never be a memory more vivid than the time I managed to seep 14 millilitres of non-dairy formula down my daughter's tiny little fledgling bird neck.

Josh: Our daughter was superb at breastfeeding, which is why I know you as a reader would prefer to hear about how badly it went with my son. He had tongue tie. From what I can tell, tongue tie didn't exist when we were kids, but now is the reason why about 98 per cent of babies with parents in East London struggle to feed. It basically means your child's tongue is tethered down to the bottom of the mouth like a tent in a hurricane. This means one of two things: either they can't create the right kind of suction to take on milk or in taking on milk they also suck in loads of air, their mouth acting like a kind of rudimentary SodaStream. My son fell into the second of these camps, so every time he fed, his stomach would inflate like a balloon, temporarily giving him the body shape of Mr Blobby (and, less amusingly, giving him such bad stomach pain that he woke up every hour of the night). And so a few weeks into his life we found ourselves taking him to a doctor who shoved a pair of scissors in his mouth and gave it a snip, like he was opening a village fete. Very occasionally with doctors you think 'this bloke is stealing a living', and this was one of those occasions. Luckily this stopped the Mr Blobby issues, although our son decided to persist with the hourly wake-ups; he was really into them by now.

Rob: Once you get through the breastfeeding/formula stage, then it's on to weaning the kids on to solids. I FUCKING HATED THIS STAGE. If I'm brutally honest, I'm not a fan of babies. I love having kids but if they could have arrived at two years of age already on solid food and potty-trained, that would be the absolute dream.

The first bit of advice I would give is for when you are on the food pouch stage (which is basically mashed-up solid food in a large Capri Sun-type pouch with a plastic screw lid). The first thing to know is don't you dare use a spoon. For no reason whatsoever I was squeezing the food pouch on to the spoon then delicately placing it in my baby's mouth. Like some Victorian member of the aristocracy being fed at a summer soiree by their butler. It's a complete waste of time; you think you are teaching them table manners. It's a baby, so they don't remember anything. Just take the lid off, shove the pouch in their gob and squeeze like you are fattening up a goose for a foie gras future. Hours of my life I wasted squeezing a pouch on to a spoon only for my daughters to smash the spoon out of my hand on to the floor. After a while you can just give the kid the pouch for them to hold and squeeze themselves. (I must add none of this is scientific advice. I do not claim to be a good dad; the only thing I can claim is that 'I am a dad' and this is how I cope.)

Josh: A lot of parents attempt to hide vegetables in their children's food to trick them into eating them. 'Oh, you think that was a slice of chocolate cake you just ate, well unlucky, there was actually an aubergine inside it.' My parents didn't do this, partly because I didn't grow up in a cartoon and partly because they had a better system of making me eat vegetables – they gave me no better option. My parents weren't just vegetarian, they were, from what I can tell, the only people in Devon in the 1990s who were into organic wholefoods. Surely I was the only child in the UK in 1994 who regularly ate tofu and considered it one of the better dinner options. Friends would come round for dinner and I would have to explain to them that while they ate Findus Crispy Pancakes at home, here they would be eating a bowl of heavily boiled vegetables that my dad called 'hippy stew'. My dad's addition that 'it's much better for your guts' not really winning them round in the way he imagined. They would rarely come back.

The fact I spent my childhood eating the world's most unappetising food makes it even more galling that my daughter spent the first few years of her life turning down foods that I would have dreamt of as a sugar-starved seven-year-old. My daughter has one simple food rule: it must be beige. I'm not sure if beige counts as one of the major food groups but if it does I'm confident it is one you shouldn't eat exclusively from. But there she is, night after night, her plate with the colour palette of a pensioner's wardrobe. And what a colour to choose for your food; imagine reducing your diet to just ten items and one of them being Jacob's Cream Crackers.

In the unlikely event my daughter finds herself on death row for murder, I fear her final meal will be plain pasta. Her ultimate staple. Why ruin that pasta by adding flavour and distracting from the main event, that unforgettable taste of flour and egg? The Italians have been messing it up for years with their sauces, no thank you, it's never a Dolmio day in our house.

This means that eating out with my daughter is always a maddening challenge as she goes off menu with less respect for a restaurant's cuisine than a British tourist on the Costa del Sol. She's the only person whose Nando's order is mashed potato and pitta bread. The only person whose order in a Pizza Express is just the base. The only person whose Wagamama order is 'Can we please leave?'

At first I tried to kick against this, fearing that while other parents at the school gates would be worrying about chickenpox or nits, I would be the only one picking up a child with scurvy. I desperately tried to convince myself that my daughter had just not found the right non-beige meal. I look back with pity at the man I was three years ago, buying recipe books with names like *100 Tasty Meals for Your Little Ones* and going to the shop to source ingredients to make her a cheese and herb frittata, confident this was the dish that would change everything. It would never change anything. In fact, if I could give you one bit of advice as a parent (and really in a whole book I should offer at least one bit of advice), it is that it is galling enough to have the dinner you made rejected, but it is 100 times worse when you have spent three hours getting the ingredients and following the recipe. Just give up hope; it's easier for everyone.

And whatever you do, don't take it personally. Which, of course, is exactly what I did. As, for about two years, I convinced myself that my daughter disliking pizza wasn't an opinion based on her taste buds but a power play and an affront to my parenting. *Who doesn't like pizza?* I'd think. *Surely it is far more likely that she likes it but just wants to torture me and ruin my life.* It is a terrible reflection of my mindset that I was far more willing to believe my child was a psycho who hated me than someone who just didn't like the taste combination of cheese and tomato. What I'm saying is that food is another element of parenting that sent me slowly mad.

Also, here's a thought you don't get in many parenting books: is this fruit and veg thing just a load of old bollocks? Because it turns out when you admit your child only eats beige food, suddenly every other parent you meet tells you they are in the exact same position. And all our kids are fine. Look at their skin, their energy levels, their growth – they're all healthier than us. I'm blowing this all apart: the healthiest possible diet you can live on is plain penne and pitta bread.

Rob: The way I look at it is as long as kids eat enough fruit and vegetables, who cares if it's the same five meals on rotation? Parents who brag about their kids that eat all sorts of foods is such an odd flex. 'Oh yes, Felix loves a Moroccan chickpea stew with harissa.' Who gives a shit? My kids are on microwavable steam veg and some sort of beige protein and carb. If they eat all the veg, they get dessert. Job done.

Josh: These days I find I'm much more relaxed about my daughter's food and this is because I have a new system for getting her to eat well. I continue to give her the World of Beige at home, but tell myself that this is fine as she gets all of her vegetables when I am not there. And I can do this because my daughter goes to a nursery in East London that may as well be called The Stiff Neck Finishing School. Consequently the meals she eats there are not just better than the food I give her at home but the food I give myself. Don't believe me? Here is a copy and paste of an email I have just been sent taking us through today's menu (as if any parent is really reading that):

- Wednesday breakfast – Toasted oats with warmed berries and yogurt
- Wednesday lunch – Spanakopita with green salad
- Wednesday dinner – Herby paneer baked rice followed by baked plums and custard

I didn't even know what paneer was until I was 35 years old. And I still have absolutely no idea what spanakopita is. Yet there she is at nursery appreciating food like she's Tom Kerridge judging the *Great British Menu*, before heading home to refuse jam on her toast as it is a bit out there. I have a terrible feeling that pizza was a power play after all.

On the other side of the coin, after the hell of tongue tie it turns out my son is an incredible eater: put it in front of him and he will attempt to get it down his throat. Well, this will be much easier, we thought, as he ate his 16th grape of the day, but as with everything in my life, it turns out this brings its own problems. I always presumed it was a myth that babies wanted to put everything in their mouths. Turns out my daughter was just being picky – she was rejecting putting a marble in her mouth in the same way she didn't want to eat plums. But my son, well, he won't just eat peas or bolognese but leave him unattended in a room for more than ten seconds and he is eating a plug, a passport or the cat. Careful what you wish for.

9

Losing Your Social Life

'When the baby first arrives there is the initial denial stage when as a young naive parent you think I'm not like those other parent losers.'

Josh: In an annoying turn of events, when we first became parents our friends carried on living their lives exactly as they had before. It turned out that it didn't matter that we were stuck inside struggling to get a baby to sleep/feed/not shit on a Babygro, they were still more than happy to meet up in a pub to drink six pints of craft lager like nothing had changed. It's almost like we were not the centre of their universe, which was a tough lesson to learn on three hours' sleep.

I will admit that I dealt badly with suddenly losing my social life. By this I don't mean I refused to accept my youth was over and continued to go out on the megalash like an awful dad in a messed-up celebrity's memoir, but simply that I took the more mentally healthy option of staying in and being really, really resentful of people that got to go out. It didn't help that I lived in a place with loads going on the moment you walked out of the door. I don't mean for kids – it is rubbish for them – but for adults that lived my old life of pubs and restaurants and, well, other pubs. It's okay for Rob.

He lives in Zone 5 and nothing happens there, so there is absolutely no temptation for him, but I live in an area where you can't even get your hair cut without being given a can of Neck Oil to get you through it.

The temptation was everywhere. When my daughter was around two months old, the only way we could get her to sleep in the evening was for me to push her in a buggy around the streets near our house. I spent my evenings that December looking through pub windows at people sharing their lovely Christmas pints, like I was a man who was down on his luck in a festive movie. *Can I walk into a pub with a baby at 10pm?* I'd think, before deciding it was probably a bad look and most importantly, Rose would kill me if she found out (and anyone who tells Rose I did go in and have a pint while our daughter slept, they are a liar and they definitely didn't see me).

Rob: When the child arrives, your life is completely turned upside down; everything you have ever done now needs to be done in a totally different way, including your social life. When I say totally different, I mean that everything that you do is now more expensive, more logistically difficult, and emotionally and physically more tiring. No more popping to the pub for a quick pint. If you want to go to the pub without the baby it will involve organising babysitters or negotiating with your partner. Which normally involves a trade-off for night out dates in the future for them.

Taking the baby to the pub with you for a quick pint involves working it around the naps and at least ten minutes of bag packing even before you work out whether to walk with the buggy or jump in a taxi. Both options prompt questions. The buggy will be too big to manoeuvre in and around the pub. If you take a taxi you will need to take a car seat for the journey. By the time you have attempted to work out all these problems you have already admitted defeat and have opened a bottle of wine to gulp down as you watch *Love Island* in silence.

Josh: My chronic and unmanageable FOMO reached its peak on the weekend of the Glastonbury Festival. Rose and I had been to every Glastonbury since we had got together, but this weekend we were going to just stay at home and watch it on TV. 'Oh, it's just as good on TV,' I told myself, not believing a word I was saying. The problem was this was just my own issue; Rose was fine with not going. Some friends who had also just had a kid suggested that on Glastonbury weekend we could meet in the park and have a glass of wine and picnic, adding, 'We can make our own fun.' 'Yes, that would be lovely,' I said, thinking, that sounds absolutely abysmal and the fact you think that would be just as good as Glastonbury makes me question who you are as people and our friendship as a whole.

When the weekend arrived, I had to admit to myself I wasn't fine with us not going to Glastonbury, however many times I looked at the sky and said, 'If anything it's actually too hot to be at a festival. I don't think I would have liked it.' If I had been fine with not going I wouldn't have banned Rose from talking about Glastonbury for the whole weekend, I wouldn't have insisted we didn't put on any radio or TV coverage of the festival in the house as it would be too painful and I wouldn't have left every WhatsApp group on which it may be discussed. To this day I still have no knowledge of what happened at the 2019 Glastonbury Festival, or even if it went ahead. However, it was that weekend when I realised that I needed to face up to it: my life had changed.

Rob: I've never been a fan of Glastonbury and other festivals. I just can't bring myself to go in the Portaloos and do a poo on a stranger's poo.

Josh: It is best just to admit it to yourself that your life has changed. You are no longer a couple, you are a trio, and that one-month-old who cannot speak is in charge of every decision. You have to make your peace with the fact that going out becomes a trade-off, and 98 per cent of the time it isn't a trade worth making. It's not about the evening, you can get a babysitter. It's about the next day, when you undertake the single worst task of parenting – looking after children with a hangover. The self-hatred, the regret, the glacially slow movement of time. Each minute feeling like an hour. Each episode of *In the Night Garden* feeling longer than *Ben Hur*. Everything driven by that distant dream of the moment when they are asleep and you can have a curry and go to bed at 8.30pm.

When some people become parents they decide that their children are just going to have to be part of their social life, and they will do all the things they used to do but with their children in tow. These people are – to be blunt – insane. You see them at weddings trying to maintain a smile as they drag a screaming child out of the church during the vows or carry them around the dance floor during 'Material Girl', pretending that spinning a dead-weight child is really cutting loose. 'We had a great time,' they tell you as they leave at 8pm for bedtime, ready to sit in a dark hotel room unable to turn on the TV for fear of waking their offspring. I have friends that this year are bringing their child to Glastonbury. Their child is 18 months old. Give it up. I don't care if you've bought some tiny ear defenders, going to a festival with a child is the single worst idea in parenting history. What was the best bit of Glastonbury? Was it trying to get a child to do their lunchtime nap in a boiling hot tent or attempting to change their nappy in a field of 100,000 people watching Paolo Nutini? Your life has changed. It's over. Come back in 15 years.

Rob: When the baby first arrives there is the initial denial stage when as a young naive parent you think I'm not like those other parent losers. Why does my life have to change? It's still me, the young, cool, sociable couple but just with a baby in tow.

You attempt to visit the new really trendy Japanese restaurant that's just opened in a converted church round the corner in the new cool bit of your local area. 'Come on, Lou, everyone is talking about it; we must go.' When you arrive there's a tiny staircase for you to carry the buggy down, no high chairs and no kids' menu. It's uncomfortably quiet and lots of slim and well-rested couples with no kids sit there flirting quietly as you try to wrangle your screaming beast offspring. Everyone is looking and rolling their eyes as they judge you. The cool 17-year-old hipster waiter hates everything about you and your baby. You have a terrible time, concede defeat and accept that you will be in Wagamama for dinner for the next 15 years of your life. Hey, I'm not having a go at Wagamama, I like it there, but there are only so many giant chicken nuggets with curry sauce and rice you can have until you start to contemplate, 'What's the point in life?'

I have contemplated this a lot more since having kids. I don't think there is a point, but I do think a couple of things make life a lot easier. Not having any opinions helps life go a lot more smoothly. Having opinions and principles really makes things harder work. If you can go through life without those two things you're on to a winner. Also accept you don't really have as much control over your life as your ego likes to tell you. Life is really hard and sometimes you get the luck and sometimes you get a shit sandwich. You can only do so much to attract or avoid either of those two things; how you react to those things is way more important.

Josh: The feeling that suddenly we were ostracised from our social group remained with us until three months later, when two of our friends told us they were expecting. Previously when people had told me they were having a baby, I'd ham up just how excited I was for them to cover up for the fact that really I wasn't that fussed either way. Now the news that our friends were expecting was the greatest news I had ever received. No longer were we alone. It was like they had defected from North Korea to join us on the side of good. (The main difference in this analogy being that in this case they had signed up to a life of far less freedom.)

'We're not going to let them take over our lives or change what we do,' they told us. 'If we want to go on a big night out we will just get a babysitter and then pump and dump the breast milk the next morning,' (they'd researched the terminology). 'If we want to go for a Sunday roast they can just come with us and sleep in their pram.' Such was their confidence in this attitude that the first thing the mum planned to do on returning from the hospital was to end nine months without an alcoholic drink with a cosmopolitan that she had left pre-mixed in their fridge. It brings me great pleasure to tell you that the cosmopolitan was poured down the sink undrunk a week into parenthood and this couple were last seen at soft play at 8am on a Saturday morning, rejigging the rooms in their house to help with sound bleed at bedtime and spending their Sundays walking their child up and down the road outside the pub while their friends had a roast inside. I often comfort myself with this in my darker moments.

Rob: If you are a drinker then the issue you will have is not the night out, but the hangover the next day. If your partner has allowed you to have the night out then it's almost certain that you will be put in charge of child duties the next day. So for every night you have to work out: is this going to be worth the hangover? Because you don't know the pain of wiping shit off your baby's arse with a hangover until you've wiped shit off your baby's arse with a hangover. Even if you didn't feel sick with your hangover before, you 100 per cent will feel sick once you've smelt it and seen it. It's something that will haunt me forever – my body and brain couldn't deal with what I had to do. I was just thinking this can't be my actual life. I feel physically broken and bilious and now this is happening to me. All the while, the most perfect, innocent and magical miracle is lying in front of me giggling and gurgling. This just makes you feel even more disgusting and pathetic thinking about how drunk you were the night before.

The way forward is daytime drinking... hear me out. Rather than meeting your mate in the pub at 8pm, go for an earlier start and earlier finish. That way you can have a few beers and be drunk between 12pm and 6pm. Then call it a night, go home and have a takeaway, drink LOTS of water, then have two pre-emptive paracetamols and you will have your hangover at about 3am when you are already asleep. You wake up in the morning groggy but human.

Josh: New Year's Day 2020 was my lowest ebb, the moment I knew I could never do it again. I went to bed at 3am, my daughter was up at 6am. Three hours before, I had been saying goodbye to my friends and drinking a pint of water as if that was going to make any difference at all to my fate. Now it was 6.15am and I was reading *Funnybones* to a two-year-old for the fourth time in a row. Thinking, *At least 2020 can't get any worse than this* (a fact I was very wrong about). There are people who can't drink certain spirits after once throwing them up, I think I am the only person who can never again read *Funnybones* because of its associations with hangover PTSD. Those skeletons on the cover looking at me like we have shared a terrible secret. The moment I hear the words 'In a dark, dark street in a dark, dark town', there I am again on New Year's Day in a dark place with a dark, dark hangover.

What made it worse was that New Year was an exception; by this point I had come to accept that I was middle-aged. And the less I went out the more I didn't want to. In fact, I was becoming excited by a new sensation: the feeling of not being hung-over. A feeling otherwise known as smugness.

Because in my twenties I wasn't someone who felt sick or unable to get out of bed after drinking, I used to think that I didn't suffer from hangovers. I thought I was just someone who was tired all the time. I presumed I probably wasn't getting enough iron or something like that. Turns out that was my hangover, and I was hung-over for a decade. Who knew? Probably everyone but me. Once again, I'm an idiot. Not now though. Now I get up each morning and I feel great – I am insufferable. You know that awful twat that tells you 'I actually have more energy since I had a child than I did before'?, well, that is me. Or at least it was me and then I had another kid. And it was back to square one. I'm broken.

Rob: However, this doesn't last forever. My children are six and four, which I like to call freedom age. I am writing this from the balcony of a hotel in Ibiza on a stag do. A stag do I was invited on two weeks ago and when I told Lou she said, 'Yeah, deffo go. You have been working hard – it'll be fun.' What a woman. Of course Lou is wonderful and pure of heart, but also the kids are much easier now. If this stag do had come up a couple of years ago, I wouldn't even have bothered asking her. Lou would have probably said okay, but in a worried and resigned way due to the prospect of her having to look after two children under the age of two for three nights looming over her. I would have felt uncomfortable as it's too much for one person to deal with, especially as I am away from home so much already with work. But now it's so much more relaxed in the Beckett house, although of course there is still a trade-off of time away. Lou is booking to go away with her mates later in the summer. Our normal rule is ideally time away should be midweek in the school term time. That way it's not too intense as most of the time the kids are in school.

Social media is the main problem as everyone's life looks

so fucking amazing, but as you know it's all lies. For example, this stag do involved a trip to Ocean Beach in Ibiza. On social media it looks like a fancy beach club with tables full of booze and beautiful bronzed Adonises and blonde bombshells. All soaking up the sun like sexy seals with their muscular tanned and smooth bodies. It's more like one of the brothels in *Game of Thrones* but outside next to a pool. Everyone is absolutely twatted and trying to shag each other. I arrived late to the stag do completely sober. It felt like a state of emergency, as if a tsunami warning had sounded and a zombie outbreak had happened at the same time. People falling over and dropping drinks, drunk people hanging off each other with hands and mouths everywhere like zombies snogging and groping each other. It was like a combination of *The Walking Dead*, *Saving Private Ryan* and *Geordie Shore*. I couldn't believe what was happening in front of my eyes. It was like the last days of Rome – something I kept saying out loud to other 'partygoers' to blank faces of zero recognition. I'm not trying to be judgemental and snobby here, I love a piss-up. Sure, I am a well-respected best-selling academic author now (☺), but I'm still a bloke who went viral for eating chicken by a bin as the police approached, who then went on to scream 'Wakey, wakey, motherfuckers' out of a cab window at midnight on a megaphone. I'm no stranger to a good old knees-up, but this was different level.

When I was chatting with numerous different drunk 'revellers', lots of them kept mentioning how nice I smelt. Sure I wear a bit of neck splash from time to time, but I wouldn't say I pride myself on my scent. I don't think I smelt particularly amazing. In fact, I hadn't showered – I had only just got off the plane, jumped in a cab, dumped my bag in the hotel, changed my top and put on some aftershave, then went to the club. But due to my late arrival to the pool party I was the only one who didn't smell of a magic combo of piss, sick, sweat and sun cream. Which led to me being the best-smelling man in Ibiza for a magical moment in time. It felt great. Who would have thought it? Bobby Beckles the best-smelling boy in the Balearics. However, it's all relative – a gazelle doesn't need to be faster than a lion to survive a hunt. It just has to be faster than the slowest gazelle. On this occasion I was definitely faster than the slowest, smelliest gazelle in Ibiza. I was the best-smelling seagull at the bin. That's the problem with Instagram – it all looks great, but you can't smell what's going on; you can only see and hear it. I've been on the front line and, let me tell you, 'insta smell' is not an update you want to see on your iPhone.

Josh: If I'm honest, sometimes I don't know who I am any more. I go to bed at 9.30pm. I turn down a glass of red wine in case I feel the effects come morning. I say things like, 'We can't start watching an episode of *Succession* at 9pm; it's an hour long, I'm not Keith Richards.' I no longer crave to go out, I don't think I could even deal with it any more. You let a dad go out on the piss and they will just end up drunk next to a bin eating fried chicken and filming themselves for Instagram – no one wants to be that guy.

On the plus side, a lot of my friends have now joined us on the boring side of the North Korean border, and that makes no longer having a social life much easier. Things are so much simpler when at 10pm on Saturday night none of us are having fun. The thing I get jealous of now isn't people going out, but just people who get time to themselves.

There is one couple we know – I'll call them Steve and Emma, because that is their names – who don't want kids, and I think about their lives whenever I'm stressed. Wondering what pointless but joyful activity they are up to at that exact moment. During lockdown, as I tried to balance recording a TV show from my attic with being locked in a house with a two-year-old, they walked into central London for something to do. Imagine that, needing to fill time. Steve is in his forties and plays *Call of Duty* in the daytime. Emma made her own Christmas crackers. Steve travels up to Old Trafford for every Man United home game even though they are never going to win the league. Emma has taken up knitting. I'm sorry, but if you have time to make your own scarf, you have too much time. Just have a bloody drink – some of us don't get to.

Rob: I don't know if it's because of the exhaustion of being a parent or that I'm getting older, but I am getting way less sociable. Which is strange as I am a naturally outgoing and sociable person. But I find socialising quite tiring when I'm not fully charged up with energy. I think the lack of sleep and demanding nature of two young kids can really drain your batteries. Plus my job is talking for 90 minutes every night on stage in front of people, which is knackering. So when I have a day off the last thing I need to do is to go out and tell some anecdotes. Whereas when I worked in the accounts department in an office on my own, filing invoices all day, I FUCKING LOVED socialising. I was that pathetic loser who hated his job and whose only outlet was showing off and trying to be funny in the pub. It was essentially a hostage situation where I would perform at people creating my own open mic gig. Thank God

I found comedy and an outlet for that energy. What a piece of shit I was and I can only imagine what kind of disgusting corporate sales lizard I would have become if I had carried on working in the city.

The thing is, now the kids are old enough that it's easy looking after them hung-over, I have actually calmed down on the drinking. I actually think I prefer staying in to going out now, especially when there is no one at home. My house is so loud and busy now that whenever I get the opportunity to sit in there on my own, I love it. I actually think sometimes about Lou breaking up with me and moving back into her mum and dad's. Obviously that would be a terrible thing to happen and it would crush me. But the first few days would be amazing, just sitting there in an empty, quiet house with the TV remote, catching up on all my favourite programmes. Ordering a pizza for one person rather than spending about £50 on buying it for four mouths. I know that enjoyment would stop after about 48 hours and then I would descend into a full emotional breakdown, but what a great first two days.

I think as you get older and become more comfortable in your own skin you don't need to be surrounded by so many people. When you're 18 and insecure and naive you have a friendship group of about 900 people. That dwindles over time. I love being with Lou and the girls and that's enough for me now. I used to need to be near and with lots of people and I needed to feel those people liked me, due to a deep-rooted feeling that I was unlikeable or not good enough, something I imagine a lot of people feel. I would have to get drunk to be confident enough to talk to those people and make them laugh and smile, so I felt good about myself. But that's not the right way to do it. Nothing external can make you feel good about yourself in the long term, it's brief dopamine hits. True self-worth can only come from within. It's something I've really had to work hard on. I used to have to be out and about socialising with people literally all the time. Entertaining them to stop the negative voices in my head telling me that I wasn't good enough. When I first started working with Romesh doing live shows and filming, I used to try and convince him to share a room with me because I didn't want to be alone. But it's exhausting being out and about and chatting to people all the time.

Having a baby is a great introduction to becoming comfortable on your own and in your own skin as when you are out and about with a baby you are essentially alone. Especially when they are really young they can't talk or laugh or even focus on you with their eyes in the first few weeks. Just this beautiful, priceless ornament that needs feeding and cleaning. You learn to work out what it is that brings you comfort on your own. Maybe a walk with a podcast on, a coffee in a nice cafe, sitting in your garden. I love the odd night out with mates now, but I'm just as happy indoors doing Lego or out for a walk on my own. There is a quote by Jean-Paul Sartre that I used to think was compete bollocks when I was young, but now as I grow older it's starting to make sense: 'Hell is other people'. But not you people reading this; you guys are great. It's those other fuckers.

But take that quote with a pinch of salt. I've just spent three nights on the San Antonio strip.

Discipline

*'It is impossible not to back down and if you don't
believe that you have the soul of a serial killer.'*

Josh: I didn't grow up in a house where discipline was a huge thing. This was due to a combination of two factors: my parents being hippies and me being a complete square. My parents had made the decision that I would be able to run free and do my own thing and I had decided to use this blank canvas to diligently do my school work and obey every rule given to me by anyone. Unlucky, hippies, I called your bluff: you've ended up bringing up a straight. The only time I remember being told off by my parents was when me and my half-brother Henry mixed all the chemicals from the loft in the bath to make a potion after we had read *George's Marvellous Medicine*. Walking into the bathroom to see us mixing up a steaming and deadly concoction, my dad, by his standards, went absolutely mental. It was a close call. Had we had a cup full of a mixture that contained anti-freeze, WD-40 and Swarfega, my dad would have lost his two sons and worse still, you would currently be reading a book about parenting by Rob Beckett and Jon Richardson, and no one wants that.

Before I became a parent, I was under the impression that discipline came down to consistency and that all these people with kids kicking off just needed to show them boundaries. Basically, I had watched two episodes of *Supernanny* in 2004 and presumed I now had it nailed. Two words: naughty step. For those of you who didn't spend the mid-noughties watching *Supernanny* (what the hell were you up to?), the naughty step is a disciplinary tactic in which parents send their children to sit on the bottom stair until they realise that it was wrong to put a Cheestring in the DVD player (I'm not sure how steps-based punishment works for those in flats or bungalows – presumably their kids just have to sit on the roof). The idea being that this moment of silent contemplation leads to reform, in the same way prison always stops people reoffending. Suffice to say, my house doesn't have a naughty step and the one time we did try it with my daughter she just called our bluff and went upstairs the moment we left her on the step. Unable to find an old episode of *Supernanny* on All4 to see what to do next, we abandoned the naughty step plan altogether.

When you become a parent, you realise that consistency is one of those things that is brilliant in theory but totally unworkable in reality, like communism or Richard Madeley hosting *Good Morning Britain*. Yes, it is easy to be consistent on paper (or in an edited documentary on Channel 4), but now it is 8.45am, you are late for nursery, your daughter is kicking off because you said she can only take two teddy bears and she wants to take a third one. You know it doesn't matter but you have said it now and so you can't back down, even though everything is going wrong just because you won't back down. You are going to be late for nursery and then you will miss a dental appointment because of it, but you will still have to pay for the appointment and not get another one for six months. Are you sticking to your guns? What I am saying is that being Supernanny is absolutely unworkable.

But we all fall for it, and there is no one as smug as those offering advice before they have children. I have a friend who, when his wife was pregnant, told me that parenting is all about consistency and that he would never back down with his child as that would just make things worse in the long run. Which I felt was quite an intense thing to say to me at his own baby shower. The last time I saw this man he was leaving his house to buy his son milk at 9pm, having half an hour earlier told him that he was going to have to go to sleep without his milk. It is impossible not to back down and if you don't believe that you have the soul of a serial killer.

Rob: One thing I remember happening when Lou was pregnant was both of us being very judgemental about the way other people raised their kids and how we would be totally different. There would be no sugar, no screens at the dinner table, no rudeness. That completely goes out of the window once you're trying to cope as a parent and barely surviving. Especially when the kids get older and start talking back at you – sleep-deprived parents haven't got a chance. I feel like a pensioner being scammed for gutter cleaning or new double-glazed windows. Just meekly sitting there nodding in agreement as a child demands more Haribo. I genuinely don't know how parents get their kids to sit at a dinner table without either some sort of device playing cartoons or colouring books and pens. People say that children being on their screens too much stops them socialising and having people skills. Well, my kids don't shut the fuck up – they will be absolutely fine socialising.

Maybe it's not the screen time, maybe you've just got a boring and awkward kid. Parents put too much pressure on themselves stopping kids having 'too much' screen time. The future of the world is in coding and the digital world. Your kid needs to know how it all works. Imagine your child going to university at 18, never having used a phone or an iPad. They will have no chance, like some 1970s market trader trying to do cash deals with no invoices. Remember when we were young, there was always a kid at school that didn't have a telly in the house. Not because they couldn't afford one but because they were so culturally elite. They were always slightly odd; same with kids that have never had a McDonald's. It's more the ego of the parents trying to prove a point than for the good of the child. People love to tell you that they don't own a telly in order to feel superior. If you dig a little deeper they always have an iPad or work computer with ITV Hub on it so they can watch *Love Island*.

Josh: Clothes are the absolute battle zone in our house. Somehow, my four-year-old has stronger views on the dos and don'ts of what to wear than Anna Wintour. This doesn't mean she dresses well. Oh no, it means she dresses like Su Pollard on a night out, but she has very strong views that she will decide on this. How can you get angry about clothes and then put on three separate items that have pictures of unicorns on? Your quality control is all over the place, mate.

I had one early stand-off where I realised that I just wasn't made for setting down rules and making my daughter abide by them. She was about two and refusing to wear her coat to go to the park. This is where I show her who's boss, I thought, and made clear we would not leave the house without her wearing her coat. If I lose this then I have lost control of everything, I told myself; next week she'll be smoking crack. An hour and a half later we were still in the hallway, she hated me, she was never going to wear her coat and I may have proven a point but I have no idea what it was. This kind of thing never happened on *Supernanny*, it couldn't – the show was only an hour long.

At this point, like all stiff necks with young children, I read that book by Philippa Perry with the long name that everyone always goes on about and IT CHANGED MY LIFE, MAN. It turned out that when your child was angry you just needed to stroke them on the nose and everything would be... of course not. You should read the whole book if you want the full explanation but basically – get this – it is quite good to treat your children as human beings and try to understand them. Now when my daughter won't wear a coat, I just say I'll take your coat and you can put it on when you want, and within a minute she is wearing it. If she won't eat her dinner I try to understand why (answer: pasta sauce). If she won't wear any of the clothes she has and we are late for nursery I will still go mental as some things are just unreasonable.

Rob has told me that his sure-fire way of maintaining discipline is to put a pompom in a jar every time his children do something good and then reward them with a present when the jar is full. When he tells me about this he speaks like he has discovered the secret to human happiness. He is one week away from telling me that he has started a pompom jar for himself and he is really behaving the best he ever has. We tried to bring in a pompom jar in our house but I messed up and bought too big a jar for the pompoms. Basically, my daughter would have had to do between 500 and 600 helpful things before she had filled the jar and earned an ice cream. And let's be honest, that wasn't much of a drive as I am so weak that she has an ice cream most days anyway when I am panicking she doesn't love me enough.

This is the problem: I am a weak man who is too desperate to be loved. I mean that is the problem in terms of discipline, although you could also apply that to most of my life. This means we try to bring in systems like Rob but we don't stick to them. We have a sticker chart that lasted from Monday to Wednesday in March 2020 and is still on the fridge, a huge jar containing six tiny pompoms (thanks, Rob!) and a clock that tells her when to wake up that has never been used.

Perhaps our lowest moment came when my daughter wanted a Bluey dolls' house and we said that in exchange she would have to give three of her toys that she doesn't use any more to a charity shop. I know what you are thinking, incredible parenting, right? Learning the value of money, how some children don't have as much as you and also that we were in charge. It was destined to be remembered as our greatest moment as parents. Until I realised last week that she has got the Bluey dolls' house and two months on we still haven't got round to taking the toys she chose to the charity shop; they remain in her bedroom. Really, really poor parenting.

Incredibly, and here is the biggest twist of the book, despite all this my daughter is a well-behaved kid, happy and well mannered. I have absolutely no idea why. Have that, Supernanny!

Rob: If your kid doesn't want to talk to you at the dinner table, don't blame them. Have a look in the mirror, be honest with yourself, maybe you're boring and your chat is shit. You're going to have to lead by example, whip out some anecdotes, have a laugh with the waiters, put in some effort. Children are bored of telling adults what they did at school. If I'm totally honest I've been out for dinner with some adults that were so dull I would have loved half an hour on my iPad if it was socially acceptable. I'm starting to think kids have the right way of thinking, it's us adults that have got it wrong. Sometimes people are boring and life is too short to waste time talking to them.

When I'm trying to lure the kids off their screens, 'Favourites' is a good game to play with them at the dinner table. My mum plays it with the girls and they love it. You go through different categories of things and ask them their favourites. Crisp flavour, colours, holidays, toys, etc. Obviously that has a shelf life but when it comes to teenagers you need to vary the questions. It's not Peppa Pig or Bluey. It's MDMA or Ket. But a conversation is a conversation, so don't be harsh on yourself. Also after a busy day arguing with each other, a dinner in silence as you choke down a lasagne while pretending to have lovely family time, accompanied by the flashing glare of four screens and headphone-strapped heads is reassuringly peaceful.

Meet the Widdicombes

Now to take us through what it is like to raise a stiff neck, Tom and Sarah Widdicombe answer your questions on what they think of their son. Due to the fact Devon is five hours from East London, these answers were submitted via email, and Josh took two days to open it as he was worried what it was going to say...

Daniela, Haywards Heath: Who is the funniest person in your family? If it is Josh, where did he get the funny gene from?

Sarah: Well, me obviously. On both counts. As you'll see.

Tom: I'd say we're all pretty funny when we get going. Having a laugh comes pretty high on the list of what we enjoy doing. One of the reasons my marriage to Sarah has held together all these years is that we laugh at each other's jokes. To be honest, though, I do quite often wonder if she is just laughing out of politeness.

Holly, Islington: What was Josh afraid of as a child?

Sarah: Mostly people he didn't know. Specifically, large groups of children at toddler groups or playgroups. We didn't have a nursery or preschool back then, just a group of mums hanging out in the WI hut, drinking tea and trying to come up with an 'activity' to keep the kids from wrecking the joint. In fact, the first time I took Josh to a toddler group was while we were still living in Bristol. He took one look at the mayhem and solemnly announced, 'Too much girls.' We left after about 15 minutes, Josh still attached to my leg, never to return.

Jane, Pennsylvania, USA: If Josh had been born female, what would you have called him? Did you have any back-up male names?

Tom: I quite liked Maud for a girl, and I also liked Arthur for a boy, but almost as soon as we saw him we both decided: Josh.

Sarah: Hmmm, I've absolutely no recollection of Maud. I'm pretty certain you've made that up.

Bonnie: Is there a specific parenting gadget that you wish you'd had when Josh was a child?

Sarah: Not really. All the usual stuff was smaller and simpler back then – Josh's buggy was about a third the size of the huge conveyances you see babies and toddlers transported in now. I had a cardboard fruit box that fitted exactly on the two thin metal slats that made up the chassis and would pile our shopping into that.

Josh was not exactly a slimline baby or toddler. (When I expressed concern to the doctor about this he replied, 'Well, you're no fighting lightweight yourself.' I'm pretty sure I cried when I got home.) Anyway, Josh point-blank refused to walk very far either, so I spent a lot of time pushing a large toddler in a tiny buggy up the steep hills of Bristol. One day, when he had just turned three and we were beginning yet another ascent of Vale Street (look it up), the buggy finally collapsed under the strain, with Josh folded inside. Luckily for him, as walking was now compulsory, we moved to Dartmoor soon after, which, unbelievably, was flatter.

Cara, Norwich: One of the trickiest problems I have with my kids is where to set the boundaries. How did you deal with this with Josh?

Sarah: I don't remember imposing many boundaries. Just safety considerations, I suppose – although Josh was never particularly adventurous anyway – and a general principle of being kind and not a pain to other people.

Someone who had almost no boundaries was my mum, Gin, who lived with us from the time Josh was three. They spent a lot of time together and were great friends. One day, when Josh was about six or seven, he'd been hassling her for one thing or another for a good half hour. Finally:

Josh: Can I have a piece of toast?

Gin: NO!!! What do you want on it?

***Ali, Sydney, Australia*: Did your son like to perform as a child? Were there any memorable performances you can describe?**

Tom: In 1997, I published my first book. Truth is I was pretty proud of it and back then I loved showing off even more than I do now, so I arranged to have a massive book launch. The idea was that we would launch the book into space in a rocket. Quite a large crowd of people gathered, thankfully everything went according to plan and no one got hurt.

After the launch, I had arranged to sell and sign books. We had a bar, fancy dress, and tea and cakes, and it was all a lot of fun. So why am I telling you this? Well, at the time I was working as a horse trainer and I had a PA system that I used for demos. I set this up at the book launch so that we could keep some kind of order. After a few minutes Josh came up and started hassling me to give him a go on the mic. I've got to be honest – I didn't want to let go of the mic myself, but I did, and off he went. He was so at home with that mic, to the point where I couldn't get it back off him and just had to leave him to it. And that's when I first got a bit of an idea what might be up ahead for Josh.

There was also a holiday where we stayed in a caravan in Wales, when the kids were really small. One evening Henry and Josh put on some kind of performance. It was a reasonable enough attempt, but – and I admit I am possibly being a bit over-critical here – I thought it could have done with a bit more happening. And of course it went on far too long.

Sarah: This is complete bollocks. I was actually six months pregnant on that holiday – with Josh. Although Henry's 'puppet show' (without puppets, if I recall) was an experience I'll never forget.

Tom: I also have to mention the film that Josh and Henry made one summer when we were on holiday in Pembrokeshire, our regular destination. This particular year, we had hired a massive Panasonic video recorder as a special holiday treat. Needless to say, I spent the whole time worrying that we were going to damage it and I would end up with a £200 bill, but thank God it all ended okay. Anyway, Josh and Henry set out to make a video of the campsite, including an interview with the proprietor, whom they had nicknamed 'Chapel Chops', or Chapel for short, on account of the campsite being next to a chapel and his massive mutton chop sideburns. As the interview was taking place, a cow and a bull started shagging right behind the fence that Chapel was leaning against. In the video, you can see the camera operator slowly re-adjusting his position to get Chapel and the cattle going at it, all in the same shot. It was an absolute winner of a film.

So all in all, looking back, it is hardly surprising that both Josh and Henry now make a living out of show business.

Hannah: What did you envisage your son doing when he was a child/teenager? Did you ever imagine him becoming a comedian?

Tom: There was a brief time when Josh was young where he wanted to be a footballer. He played a couple of games for

Bovey Tracey under-11s. It quickly became apparent that this was never going to be a viable career option, mostly due to a lack of skills, but also because it was just too much hassle. This was quite interesting for me because these were exactly the same reasons my football career never took off either.

But what came next did briefly look like it might be a goer: Josh signed up to learn to be a referee. After a few weeks, he got his qualification and bought himself the black kit, the whistle, the notebook, and the red and yellow cards.

It was my job to take Josh to the matches. I didn't find this a particularly enjoyable experience. In fact, I spent the whole time freaking out, worrying that he would make a wrong decision. I think the rules were that you weren't allowed to referee kids older than yourself. That sounds quite reasonable, doesn't it, but what they don't tell you is that on the touchline are all the kids' parents, and a 14-year-old referee is fair game in their eyes. In one match, Josh made a questionable offside decision and one of the parents stormed on to the pitch and started shouting his mouth off at Josh. I was standing on the sideline shitting myself and thinking, *What the fuck do we do now?* Anyway, Josh got out his red card and sent the guy off. Bloody brilliant!

I might be misremembering this, but I think the same guy carried on shouting from the touchline and the next thing that happened was Josh came over with his red card and ordered him out of the ground. For the next couple of matches I had to phone in sick for Josh, and then after that he decided he didn't want to be a referee any more.

Verity, Northamptonshire: What was your reaction when Josh told you he was going to pursue a career as a comedian, given that it is not a traditional career path?

Tom: When I found out Josh had done a five-minute open mic spot I was really surprised. I was amazed he had the balls, to be honest – it's a pretty brave thing to do.

In the early days, I followed his career quite closely. It was interesting watching him learn. Quite a few months in I took him to do a gig in Falmouth – a ten-minute slot in the middle of three. I watched from the side of the stage and thankfully it went quite well. Another time, I took him to a gig at the Barbican in Plymouth. He had the compere spot and the venue was packed. That evening I think he got paid £25, which covered his train ticket down from London. An old guy standing next to me, who didn't know I was his dad, said, 'He's the funniest one here tonight. I reckon he might make it.' I remember thinking how I couldn't really tell if he was any good or not. It was difficult for me to look at the situation objectively.

What really surprised me was how long it took before he started to make any money out of it. For a couple of years he was basically running at a loss just to get the airtime in and learn the trade.

Sarah: He hedged his bets by keeping the day job for a while.

Angharad: Do you actually find Josh funny?

Tom: He is funny, no question – the utter desperation in our family to have a laugh meant that it was really only a matter of time before someone got lucky and made a few quid out of it.

Sian, Canberra, Australia: Have you ever used the fact that Josh is your son to get an advantage? Did it work or fail spectacularly?

Tom: It is virtually impossible not to take advantage of being Josh's dad. It happens automatically, in so many ways, but it can cut the other way too. It's surprising how often people come up to me and say, 'I saw Josh on telly the other night. I really don't find him funny at all.' When that first happened it totally disarmed me. I was upset for a second or two, until I worked out what was going on. Nowadays I just agree and say things like, 'Yeah, it really amazes me how someone so mediocre has managed to make such a successful career out of telling a few crap jokes,' or, 'Yeah, it's amazing how someone could have a dad as funny as me and yet be so fucking unfunny themselves.' They usually just fuck off after that.

As to the advantages of being Josh's dad – well, I have to say that I do struggle politically with privilege, so I tend to feel a bit exposed when I end up being invited to gigs or getting good seats (sometimes for free) just because I am Josh's dad.

Through Josh, I have met a couple of my all-time comedy heroes – thank God it turned out they are both really lovely people, which was a huge relief for me. Nothing worse than meeting someone you are a huge fan of only to find out they are a total tosser.

I've been to Home Park (Plymouth Argyle) with Josh for a few media gigs, which has been great. You get to hang out and chat with the management team – you know, discuss tactics and so on. Even better, I've been to Anfield twice, which is without question my best football experience ever. Once, we had really good seats in the new stand – it was really great and, even better than that, we won.

It's the unseen stuff that I find really interesting. I know for a fact that some people take a different view of me simply because they are aware my son is well known. I'm not sure how I feel about that – not 100 per cent comfortable for sure – but there's really nothing that I can do about it anyway. I try not to use that privilege for my own ends, but in all honesty sometimes it's virtually impossible not to.

Ultimately, it's difficult not to feel some validation as a parent for how your kids turn out in life. But a huge caution here: if you are going to take the credit when things go right, then you also have to take the blame when things go wrong. My advice is don't go in too strong with either of those options.

Ciara: Have you ever been out with Josh and he's been recognised?

Tom: The best thing that ever happened was when we went to watch Argyle play at Anfield. Before the match, we went into a pub called the Flat Iron. It was crowded with Liverpool fans, and as soon as they clocked Josh the whole pub started singing, 'There's only one Jimmy Tarbuck.' Quickly followed by a beautiful rendition of, 'There's only one John Bishop, only one John Bishop,' and so on. I know a lot of people struggle with the whole Liverpool thing, but myself, I've bought right into it!

Laura, Brentwood, Essex: How did you feel when you found out your son was expecting his first child?

Sarah: Thrilled. My first grandchild!

Tom: Bit overwhelmed as I already had nine.

Beth: How is becoming a grandparent different to becoming a parent?

Sarah: Not having to give birth is obviously a colossal bonus.

Ed (dad to Isaac and Florence), Sheffield: What parenting habit, trait or saying do you recognise in Josh that he may have picked up subconsciously from your parenting?

Tom: One of the nicest things for me is when I see the way Josh and Rose (and lots of young parents these days, actually) are with their kids. They seem to naturally stand back and give the kids their space. For me as a parent, this was, and still is, a huge deal. I will forever be grateful for all the freedom that my mum gave me in my life. I felt no undercurrent of expectations and had total support from her throughout all of my crazy adventures. I don't remember ever feeling any pressure from her to achieve anything or to be anyone special at all.

I have tried really hard to be that way with all my kids, and now with all my grandkids. With my first family, I really didn't want to send the kids to school but the pressures at that time were more than I could deal with. So my plan was to counteract any values picked up at school with an even stronger set of values at home. Some years later, when Josh got to school age, I went along with sending him to school, partly because it was a tiny village school and partly because I didn't really realise that there was an alternative. To counteract the messages coming through school, especially secondary school, I made sure that Josh knew there was no pressure from me for him to achieve anything at all, ever.

I remember going to a parents' evening one time and one guy was saying that it would really help Josh if we did this and that. I just replied that I didn't really buy into that way of looking at life. It all got very awkward. I wouldn't be as gobby nowadays but back then I kind of viewed school as the enemy.

Ellie, London: **What is the best and worst thing about having grandchildren?**

Tom: Best thing: it's just nice to hang out with them.

Sarah: The best is that they are both already absolute legends. The worst is that living where we do, we don't get to see them often enough. We didn't see our granddaughter for over a year during Covid lockdowns, which is a long time in a small child's life and was absolutely gutting.

Actually, the worst is that you are fairly certain you won't get to see them grow beyond young adulthood. My mum died before Josh had even done his first open mic spot. She was a writer and actress, and enjoyed anything and everything showbiz. She'd have bloody loved to see what has happened to Josh.

Hannah: What single thing has Josh done which has made you the proudest?

Tom: I would say one of Josh's biggest achievements is that he is quite good at pool. I bought a table when Josh was about five. He would put the Paul Simon album *Graceland* on the turntable and spend hours practising pool. He had a chair that he carried around the table, positioning so he could reach each shot. He was utterly determined to get the hang of it. Later on, as a teenager, he had an ongoing tournament against our good friend, John Daly. It lasted for several years. I think the score ended up somewhere in the region of 224 games to 212.

Sarah: When Josh was about 12, for some homework or other he had to say how he would like to be remembered. He wrote: 'I would like to be remembered as a good bloke and a lifelong supporter of Plymouth Argyle.' I loved that.

Karen, Reading: Is there anything that Josh does that really annoys you?

Tom: Sarah's side of the family have this really strong work ethic and Josh has it too. Sometimes it's really hard for him to just hang out. I wouldn't say that it is annoying though, let's just say I've noticed it.

Laura, Brentwood, Essex: **What has been your parenting highlight?**

Sarah: One of them would definitely be Josh's speech at his and Rose's wedding, where he talked about his dad and me in very much the same way as Tom talks about his mum.

Holidays

*'Now imagine holding a 10kg bag of sugar for four
and a half hours that wriggles, kicks, screams and
shits for four and a half hours.'*

Rob: Don't bother until your youngest is at least four years old. End of chapter.

Josh: The simple fact is that going on holiday with small children is less relaxing than your actual life. You should not be looking forward to going back to work so you can chill out a bit. I am currently looking at pictures of Rob at Disney World on Lou's Instagram and he looks a broken man. Looking at how he has deteriorated over the ten days of holiday is like looking at those 'compare and contrast' pictures of Tony Blair before and after he was in power (but with less guilt about potential war crimes). In these photos Rob looks like what he is – a man who has decided to spend his fortnight off living purely on hot dogs, filling two children with e-numbers, dragging them from queue to queue in a hellish palace of capitalism and all this after altering everyone's body clocks by five hours as a little starter. And I know when he gets back he will claim it was the best two weeks of his life. And I won't believe him. (Edit – It is now a week later and this did happen.)

The thing about working with Rob is you feel instantly like you don't take enough holidays. That you, like him, should also be going away 16 times a year. I have begun to question if Rob actually likes living in Zone 5 as much as he claims, seeing as he makes sure that his family never spend more than three weeks there at a time. In fact, I'm starting to suspect that Rob isn't actually a British citizen at all and is here on a temporary holiday visa, not allowed in the country for more than 90 days a year. Whatever the truth, I expect Rob to have far more stories for this chapter than I do. Although I will be submitting my sections first because the Judith Chalmers of podcasting is still in a three-hour queue for Space Mountain with two children in Minnie Mouse T-shirts.

Rob is the kind of person that knows when the Easter holidays are going to be. The kind of weirdo who loves his time away so much that he makes holiday friends. Going for drinks with strangers and then exchanging numbers so they can meet up back in the UK, even though he knows this won't happen as he is never in the UK long enough. Rose and I are the kind of people who ignore strangers at all costs on holiday. Controversially we see those ten days on a beach as being about relaxing rather than trying to make small talk with a couple from Chepstow who work selling pharmaceuticals.

Don't get me wrong, I'm not a monster, I take my family on holiday. Sometimes you need a break, even if it is a break from the elements of your life that take the pressure off on a day-to-day basis. Things like nursery, television, stair gates, grandparents and a bed your child is comfortable sleeping in. Essentially, holidays with the under-threes are pure undiluted parenting, like glugging back straight squash. Which if you go to Disney World is also the kind of thing your children will be drinking, just to add to your troubles.

Let me take you through our family holiday to Greece when my daughter was a year old. Our week began by packing a suitcase that included 21 bottles of follow-on milk as that was the only milk she would drink. Losing this suitcase space was a particular issue for me as due to my stiff neck I have to take my own pillow on holiday to stop myself from seizing up. This meant that if I wanted to be able to look to the left for my week in Greece, I had to cut down drastically on what I was packing. Sticking purely to toiletries and minimal clothing meant I was unable to pack my copy of *Great Expectations*, another opportunity missed.

Next came the joy of a three-hour plane journey, although with a one-year-old I think it is best not to think of this as one simple three-hour chunk, but instead a mere 180 different minute-long activities:

- Play with my keys – one minute
- Play with the life vest thing without trying to set it off – one minute
- Give her some carrot puffs – one minute
- Walk her up and down the aisle without trying to piss people off – one minute
- Show her some *Mr Tumble* on a phone (before people near us become so pissed off we have to turn it off) – 30 seconds
- It comes to something when you are delighted that you can smell shit because it means you can go to the toilet to change a nappy – FIVE WHOLE MINUTES

The whole thing feels like one of those feats of human endurance people do because they weren't loved as children. Like David Blaine in that Perspex box. Although you have to question how much of a challenge that actually was. I'd have had a lot more respect for him if he had been in that box with a one-year-old. Although actually, that might have been quite creepy.

Perhaps we should have realised it wasn't going to be the same when just after we booked our holiday we asked my brother what it had been like when he went away with his three-year-old daughter. We presumed he would give it a Paul McCartney-style double thumbs up; after all, according to his Instagram it was a magical combination of swimming pool frolics and Bermuda shorts. He looked at us with the faraway stare of a man who has just come back from 'Nam and he said nothing. It turns out holidays may look the same as before on social media, but that is where the similarities stop. The departure lounge is no longer a place to get the holiday started by having a beer in a Wetherspoons, it is a place to chase a child around Currys while your partner heads to Pret to stock up on flight snacks. The beach is no longer a place to relax, but an infinite arena of potential pain for your offspring – from the burning sun in the sky to the sand that for some reason your toddler wants to try to eat. And of course the restaurant isn't a place for romantic meals stretching into a second bottle of wine, but a place where you take it in turns to eat alone while your partner pushes the Yoyo (they fold up as hand luggage!) around the block in an attempt to get your child to sleep.

In an incredible sign of how far I had misjudged our holiday to Greece, I had planned to use the break to propose to Rose (yes, until this point we had been living in sin). There is, after all, no better place to hide an engagement ring for your wife than in a suitcase of 21 follow-on milks. Halfway through the holiday with our daughter asleep, we sat outside our villa and relaxed for perhaps the first time. This is the moment, I thought, nothing could be more romantic – just us, a bottle of rosé and a baby monitor. I went down on one knee (natch), proposed, Rose said yes (phew), we both cried (predictably) and then the baby monitor burst into life with another crying human. Had our daughter heard us? Did she oppose this union? Or was it, as felt more likely, that the Greek travel cot was as comfy to lie on as a freshly gravelled driveway? It was the mattress, and she would not be going back to sleep in there anytime soon. I don't know what you did on the night you got engaged, but we slept with our daughter in between us in our bed, wondering at what point it was on holiday that Rob Beckett made all these friends.

Rob: I mean, you can take babies on holiday but it's not a holiday. When they are four and they can play in the shallow pool, that's when you start to have holidays again. This is when I make all my holiday friends as you are just standing in the sun for eight hours in knee-high water watching your kids play. My normal plan is I drink two ice-cold beers then I get bored and chatty. Before I know it, I've got six new mates that I'm going to the bar with later to watch the football. When they can play in the pool semi-unaided, that's when you feel like you're on holiday. Before that it's just looking after kids in a hotel or villa that has nothing you need in it and loads of sharp edges and hard floors. I don't know how Spanish kids survive – their hotels and villas are deathtraps. Everything is rock hard or pointy. We took our eight-month-old child to Spain in August and it was far too hot so she overheated as soon as we went outside.

I would genuinely recommend days out and mini breaks in the UK with babies and toddlers. Flying is a nightmare plus babies always get ill and trying to find a doctor on holiday is as difficult as getting a mortgage with cash deposit and no proof of income, even with a potential *Mock the Week* appearance in the pipeline. Save your money and go big on holidays when they are older and can watch a device for three hours on the plane/in the car.

If you travel with a child that's under two on an aeroplane, you have to hold them. Just hold them on your lap for however long the flight is. We went to Tenerife, which I thought was Spain and a cheeky two-hour flight. However on the runway I was informed by the pilot that it's not a two-hour flight and it's not an island off the coast of Spain; it's an island off the coast of Africa and it takes four and a half hours. That's nine episodes of *Emmerdale* back to back. If you jump in the sea in Tenerife and swim in an easterly direction, you don't arrive in Madrid, you arrive at the Western fucking Sahara. So that meant I had to hold my one-year-old for four and a half hours sitting in a seat with nothing to do, see, watch or listen to. Imagine holding a 1kg bag of sugar for four and a half hours; annoying and cumbersome, isn't it? Now imagine holding a 10kg bag of sugar for four and a half hours that wriggles, kicks, screams and shits for four and a half hours. Is this some sort of prisoner-of-war torture? No, it's your holiday that's cost you two grand.

Save your money and stay at home.

Josh: I have hope, as our children get older, that the holidays will become as magical as the ones of my youth, ones that are the reason the smell of sun cream still makes me feel happy. Holidays stop being about where you go and become about having time to just be with your family, and I should know that because every year we would go camping in Wales. Everything was perfect on holiday. Even the bad things that would happen would be deemed glorious in the myths of our family. The time we stayed in a camper van and my brother ate too much watermelon, pissed himself in his sleep and accidentally soaked my mum's foot below. The time my sister fell in the canal and my dad shouted, 'Get the camera!' The time I got a stomach bug and had to crawl out of the tent in the middle of the night holding vomit made 98 per cent of Sugar Puffs in my mouth to save the tent from ruin. ('The most heroic thing you have ever done' – my brother.) Those were great memories and one day my family will get to make their own like this. But I am absolutely not going to Disney World.

And Then There Were Two

'A few days ago, I needed a piss for three hours but just couldn't find enough time to go.'

Josh: Last week I was at a birthday party with my mate Chris, who is expecting his second child in a couple of weeks. Rather than our usual chat about Wayne Lineker's Instagram, Chris used this opportunity to earnestly ask me if having two kids really is that different from having one. I made it clear to him that it absolutely was and to enjoy his easy life now. Although for some reason this didn't seem to be the answer he wanted, and so throughout the night I heard him asking four different people the same question, desperate for a different answer. He never got it. And it was great to hear – he's had it easy for too long.

Perhaps the worst personality trait I have developed since having a second child is a seething resentment towards people with one child and how easy their life is. There is someone I follow on Instagram who does stories about how tough it is being the mother to a toddler. I used to love these posts (even more than Wayne Lineker's), chuckling to myself about how she had really nailed the unique troubles of adapting to life as a parent. Now, however, whenever I watch these stories all

I can think is: 'You have one child, you know nothing. You don't know how easy you have it.'

To be honest, I find it mad that for the first six months of the podcast Rob put up with me complaining about how difficult it was having one kid in lockdown. Acting like I was Nelson Mandela imprisoned on Robben Island, rather than a man dealing with a generally easy child who had a two-hour nap every day. Rob, I would like to take this opportunity to apologise publicly, I was in the wrong. And the best thing about this apology is I know you won't even read my bits for this book so will never see it. On that subject, when your beard gets too big, you look like the Honey Monster – what do you think about that?

Rob: When I was having a catch-up with Josh during the writing of this book, one of the first things he said to me was, 'I've got so much to say about how hard it is having two children instead of one.' But at the time of writing my kids are six and four, two daughters with slightly different personalities that, luckily, at this moment in time, gel perfectly. They can play together for hours without getting bored or wanting any other children or adults involved. It's fucking glorious. In the summer holidays I fill the paddling pool full of water and sit on a chair in the sun for hours. No other kids to look after, no other parents scrambling for small talk as our kids play. Just me, sitting sunbathing with the sound of my children splashing and laughing in the background. Sometimes I have one headphone in my ear listening to a podcast or some music. I don't even have to get up to make them a drink or get them an ice cream as the six-year-old can open the fridge and freezer herself. It's an incredible way to live your life. Josh on the other hand with his much-younger children is having a terrible time.

I am not saying this to be smug or gloat, I am trying to inspire hope, as I was once that lost, hopeless dad wondering when it will end. There is light at the end of the tunnel but at the moment for poor old Josh he is going to be stuck in that pitch-black tunnel for at least another three years minimum, and maybe up to seven more years if he rolls the dice on a third kid.

Josh: Rob repeatedly tells me this, that when your children get to a certain age, having two actually makes your life easier as they start to look after each other. An argument that feels a bit like those weird people who don't use shampoo telling you that after a while your hair actually cleans itself. This feels a long way off for us (both children and hair-wise); at the moment having two kids feels like an eternal logic problem. To have a shower involves setting out a timetable three days in advance to make sure it tallies with naps, nursery and your partner not being out of the house buying milk. A few days ago, I needed a piss for three hours but just couldn't find enough time to go. Suddenly everything you used to do seems hilariously unachievable, except ordering a Deliveroo, which becomes far, far too easy (personal best, six nights in a row).

I should add that I am aware some people don't stop at two. There are almost certainly people reading this book with three, four or five children thinking 'you pathetic couple of wankers, you're complaining about nothing'. If you are one of those people, the only thing I can say is: you only have yourself to blame, you got yourself into this mess and I have no pity for you.

Rob: While it is definitely easier as they get older, there are new challenges. They are getting bigger and ultimately they become more intelligent – much like the evolution of velociraptors in the *Jurassic World* franchise. I'm starting to lose my intellectual power over them and the problem with having more than one child is they gang up on you. One will distract you while the other puts their vegetables in the bin, things like that. They both pull me up on my accent and tell me to pronounce the 't' in water. They both also run in opposite directions when it's bedtime, knowing that if I'm parenting alone I can't grab both of them at the same time to take them up to bed.

I doubt my kids will ever have the street smarts that I learnt from my life experiences. They will almost definitely be polite middle-class adults that will be far too trusting of people whereas I can sniff out a wrong'un chancer a mile off. What they lack in the street they will make up for in the classroom. They will dominate me academically and intellectually. I hated school with a passion and they are both loving it. Recently my eldest scored 100 per cent in a maths exam. There is no way she can be mine, and if you think I am over-exaggerating for effect, then watch me on *8 Out of 10 Cats Does Countdown*. I am officially the worst *Countdown* player of all time on both versions of the show. When Lou told me about the test score I didn't feel pride, I felt worry. I immediately starting thinking, *Who has Lou been shagging when I'm on tour?* Getting jiggy with a maths nerd like Brian Cox, flirting over quadratic equations and having it off while I'm grafting away in Halifax. Before I congratulated my daughter I demanded a paternity test, which came back full Beckett zero Cox. Which was a relief to me but did spoil the moment for my daughter when I announced the paternity test results at her school prize-giving assembly.

Josh: The received wisdom is that with your second child you are more laid-back. Not in general, just in terms of how you relate to the baby. In actual fact I am the most uptight I have ever been. If I was to write a list of the most laid-back periods of my life, the first year of having two children would be laughably far from the top three. A top three which, if you are interested, looks like this:

1. The semester at university when I realised that if I picked certain modules I could have all of my lectures on a Tuesday, giving me a full six days off every week.
2. The week I did work experience at my uncle's fruit and veg shop.
3. Every holiday I went on before I had a child.

In fact, were I to choose the least laid-back moments of my life, I would say the last 18 months contained quite a few candidates for the top spot. The time when I had to hold my newborn for the whole of England's first game at Euro 2020, unable to cheer when we scored in case I woke him. The time my daughter was up ill at 3am and I knew my son was getting up at 4am to start his day. Every bedtime since the day he was born. It's either one of those or the time when I thought I was going to fail my degree because I had chosen a module I didn't understand purely because it was on a Tuesday.

What people mean about you being laid-back with your second child is that you are far less stressed about the actual parenting. A view I completely subscribe to, particularly if by laid-back, you mean worryingly lax. With our daughter we bathed her every night, with our son we told ourselves that if we don't get to shower every day then why should he? With our daughter we did the required three tummy time sessions a day, with our son we did it about once a week (meaning he may never be able to do whatever tummy time is meant to do for him). With our daughter we wouldn't let her play with the kitchen knives, with our son... I'm joking, we were (relatively) strict on that.

Maybe this isn't a bad thing for him. After all, everyone has met an only child who has been made unbearable by a lifetime of their parents doting on them. I know I have, I am one. Well, there's no such worries here. Here is a child who at the age of one is already ready to face up to a life in which you have to learn to lift your head up off a play mat all on your own.

Rob: In the dark tunnel days when you have a baby and a toddler, every second of your day is taken up by childcare, but part of the problem is that it's not the same type of childcare. It's two opposite kinds of childcare. It's like looking after a racehorse and one of those tired-looking old Blackpool donkeys. Two similar beasts with very separate needs. It's insane.

Just over four years ago, Lou and I had two children under the age of two, which meant we had to switch between the physically exhausting but fairly brain-dead activity of caring for our baby and the demands of a tiny little dictator that knows exactly what she wants but without the vocabulary to ask for it. I'm not saying caring for a baby isn't hard, it's brutal, but you're more of a production line factory worker. It's very formulaic: you feed the baby, change the baby, the baby sleeps (sometimes), then repeat. When it came to our older kid it was less demanding on the body but the mind got a workout. We'd be up all night trying to get the baby to sleep. Then out of nowhere at 6am I'd be sitting on the edge of our child's bed trying to talk to our toddler who was sad because one of her friends at nursery said that they aren't her 'pinky promise bestest friend in all the world any more'. Which physically is easy as you're just sitting on the bed, but mentally it's exhausting as you scramble for the right words and advice to give to your child. My advice, by the way, was: 'Fuck her off, you don't need her anyway, mates come and go. It's not a problem,' but in slightly more delicate language.

I find it terrifying and fascinating when I see people with five children. It must be horrendous. How do you keep them all alive? You can't cross the road with all of them properly as you literally run out of hands. You have to have a massive weird car and all holidays cost about 200 grand. I found the second so much easier than the first, but does it carry on getting easier? The third one is easier than the second. The fourth one is a breeze compared to the third. Maybe by the fifth one, it is so easy compared to the fourth you don't even realise they are in the house; it's just another body that needs clothing and feeding. Does it become like livestock? No one only has two sheep, so once you've got five, why not have another 33?

Josh: The biggest thing I didn't prepare myself for with having a second child was that just because a pregnancy went to plan the first time around it didn't mean that would happen again. When we went for the initial scan with our first pregnancy I had approached it with a deep worry – terrified something would be wrong, or that all would be fine but I just wouldn't be able to make out the baby on the screen (which, of course, was what happened). This time, buoyed by our first pregnancy and the fact we had conceived again relatively easily, I just presumed we had the knack for this kind of thing and attended our first scan with the carefree attitude of someone popping out for an all-you-can-eat breakfast.

'I'm afraid the foetus isn't the size I would expect it to be at this stage of the pregnancy,' said the man doing the scan, hoping we would read between the lines as to where this was headed. It's strange how quickly something that was filed in your mind under joy and happiness can suddenly transform into a sadness that makes you feel physically sick. Like being dumped out of nowhere by the person you knew you were spending the rest of your life with.

Offering a life raft for our hopes to cling on to, he told us that it might be that we had got the dates wrong and we weren't as far gone as we thought, but if we came back in a week we would know for sure. I think we both already knew for sure. The following week dragged slowly through day upon day of hollow positive chat, looking for hope in the minor, overanalysed details. Was the fact that Rose felt sick a sign the baby was growing and everything in fact was well? Was her nausea the same as the last pregnancy that turned out fine?

In the surgery we were both strangely calm as the bad news was delivered to us, lost in the shock of it and perhaps the odd feeling that you should keep it together in front of a man with a medical degree. Once we got on the street, Rose burst into tears and I didn't know what to say to comfort her. I am someone who defaults to looking for a solution or a way of making things feel better, but these things didn't exist.

You would presume this was the lowest moment and then day

by day it got a little less painful but that wasn't how it worked out. Having been advised that it was better to let the foetus leave the body naturally rather than undergo a procedure, a few days later Rose had to deliver the unborn foetus into our toilet while in excruciating stomach pain. We were told that perhaps this experience would offer a closure. It offered the most harrowing two hours of our lives, and I still can't really think about what Rose went through that night – it is tough to comprehend how she has had to deal with it.

There was no closure. I know I still felt the things I was feeling before. That I was a failure. That by being too confident I had somehow brought this on myself. Or that by being less confident I would have at least been more prepared for what happened, as if being prepared for a miscarriage would somehow make it just another day.

In conversations about parenthood it is still something I fear coming up and will unnaturally and awkwardly steer away from the moment it appears on the horizon. Even in writing the word miscarriage now I almost flinch, having to stop myself from using a more euphemistic phrase like 'what happened to us' in an attempt to not fully engage with it.

I remember a few weeks after it happened, Rob asking if we would have a second kid and I flat-batted the question away by garbling something about the stress of one being enough. Thinking *Why can't you just say it?* but knowing it wasn't even an option. A few weeks later, at 1am, drunk with Rose ('we might as well just get drunk now, nothing to stop us!'), I texted him to tell him. Ashamed that this was the only way I could ever see myself telling him. What a text for him to wake up to four hours later when his daughters got up. Quick check of the football headlines, check Twitter, offer condolences for a friend's miscarriage.

I am maybe trying to paint this as a time of great sadness, but the worst thing is there was probably more anger than sadness in me. I wasn't ready for how much I hated people that this hadn't happened to. How much rage I felt towards friends who then told us they were expecting a child. A feeling of 'How dare they. Why couldn't they just wait another year to spare our feelings?' Ignoring their texts about mundane things – going for a drink, the latest episode of *The Apprentice* – because I didn't want to engage with their existence, or perhaps just to somehow cause them a tiny bit of the hurt I was feeling.

We were lucky in that Rose got pregnant again and this time it was okay. One thing people didn't tell me was how much the miscarriage would destroy the experience of the next pregnancy. Suddenly a pregnancy wasn't a reason for excitement but 270 days in which we could worry it was all about to go wrong. Scans are not incredible moments of connection with an unborn son but a reminder of how it could all instantly be taken away from you by a man in surgical gloves. Some of my most vivid memories of this pregnancy were the times we would sit in the park outside the hospital waiting to go in for our scans, for which we were always far too early – maybe in an attempt somehow to engender good karma. Sitting drinking tea having convinced ourselves it could only be bad news, that from now on we were unlucky people, the kind of people these things happen to as history repeats itself.

One in four pregnancies ends in a miscarriage. It doesn't feel like that, but that is because those of us it happens to often don't like to talk about it. Why would you bring it up with people when, understandably, they don't know what to say? With the best of intentions, friends would reply to the news with comments that somehow just made it worse: 'Well, at least you got pregnant' – as if that is a consolation – or 'You said it didn't feel like the time before, didn't you?' – unintentionally implying that somehow we knew it was going to happen from the off. Consequently, one of the strangest things to come out of miscarriage is the bond you suddenly build with people who have been through the same thing. Turning your shared loss into the membership requirements of some strange exclusive club. The guy on the stag do, the friend of a friend, the comedian you never really liked. Suddenly you are all in on a secret that only you understand.

I've just read this back and it is all a little bleak, isn't it? But then I think it probably was at the time, I haven't got a huge amount of stand-up material out of it. However, as weird as it sounds, I don't wish it hadn't happened. I'm really happy in my life now (despite what you may have gleaned from this book) and if it hadn't been bad news that day I wouldn't have my son, whose two-teethed smile makes me anxious with how much love I feel every morning when I go into his room. We have now almost mythologised it as that thing we had to go through to get our second child.

When it happens you tell yourself that this will change everything, you now understand how special having a child is, you will never again take them for granted. Then it is night two, you have brought your second child home, he won't sleep and you can't believe this is happening again. You catch yourself saying that having a two-day-old child is the worst thing that has ever happened to anyone. And in your head, in that moment you completely mean it. You have learned nothing.

INTERLUDE 4

Josh and Rob
Interview
Rob's Parents

Now, we meet Rob's parents, Dave and Sue, who met up with Josh and Rob in Rob's living room to humiliate Rob for an hour. If you would like to hear this, it is included in the audiobook.

Josh: Hello. The guests we've always dreamed of, Sue and Dave. I think people will first want to know, do you think that my shoes are too dirty to do this interview?

Sue: I think you could do with a proper pair of shoes, something a little bit more substantial.

Rob: Not to make an awkward start, but I think Mum and Dad have always slightly not liked you because you beat me in the Leicester Comedian of the Year competition in 2010. Since then, I think you've held a slight grudge.

Sue: And there was one other thing as well. Do you remember when you got those pants out, on *Would I Lie to You?* It was a pair of pants you'd had a very long time and I thought you should have thrown them away before.

Rob: So, you don't like his dirty shoes. You don't like the fact he beat me in a competition, and he's got dirty pants.

Sue: But I think he's thrown them away now and I've warmed much more to him.

Josh: Oh, that's good. Right. Well, let's go for the first question from a listener to the podcast. This is from Susie, from Leicester, where I beat you, Rob. That's a coincidence. Was Rob funny as a child?

Sue: Yes, he was. And so were his brothers. It was a very fun house. Everybody was funny, but he was funny, yes.

Dave: If anybody said anything funny, he used to write it down. Especially if I said something really funny or I swore, it'd be put down in a book.

Josh: You're stealing jokes early on?

Rob: I remember buying that book. A book bought in... How old was I when we went to Cyprus? Maybe at

16, 17. It was a little blue book. I remember because I've still got it, actually.

Sue: Didn't Debbie see you writing in it over the park? You were in the park, writing in this little book.

Rob: When I did my first gig, I didn't want to tell anyone. So I was walking around the local park, practising my set. But my mum's mate, Debbie, saw me from the window and told her.

Sue: And he'd just broken up with a girl. So she said, 'I've just seen Rob over the park, sitting on a bench with a book. Do you think he's all right?'

Dave: She thought he was sulking.

Rob: Oh, yeah, with a book. Panic alert. A working-class person with a fucking book. Debbie, have you seen? He's got a book. Is everything right at home? You'd rather me have four cans of cider, it would be more normal?

Josh: So, when Rob was a child, he was funny. But were you thinking, we've got comedian on our hands there?

Sue: No, not really. No. My dad was a funny man.

Rob: To be fair, growing up, everyone was loud, and had an anecdote, and a funny angle on things. And it was like a living panel show in my own house. So I didn't feel like I was funny at all. But we were all funny. My brother, Dan, is a comedy writer now as well. It's just how everyone was. Aunties and uncles.

Sue: I think Joe tried stand-up as well. And he's funny, but he didn't like the stand-up bit.

Rob: Yes, my brother Joe is funny. And he did stand-up. But he's not got that need for attention. But I was the middle child, so I think that's why I'm the one that does it.

Josh: Did Rob have a need for attention?

Dave: Yeah, definitely.

Josh: Did he do school plays and stuff?

Sue: No. He wasn't theatrical in that way. Really, his early years were all football. That's what he did. That's where he got his energy, and his passion was football. So he wouldn't have had time to do panto or anything.

Josh: This is from Alison from Worcester. What would Rob's name have been if he was a girl?

Sue: Well, he would've been called Charlotte or Emily. They were the girls' names I had.

Josh: And did you want a girl? Because you already had boys.

Dave: I don't know. I didn't think of it at the time, but now I've got grandchildren, and I'm quite used to it, but I think I prefer boys. Boys are much easier than girls.

Rob: That's good to know about my two daughters. Oh, a lovely chat this is. What's the problem with my kids then? What's the issue?

Dave: First one, getting up at half past five in the morning and jumping on me when I stay the night.

Josh: But, I need to know about this half four thing that I've heard a rumour about?

Sue: Oh, every day.

Rob: So, this is when I used to wake up?

Josh: For how long?

Sue: Well, till he went to school. And then he always got up early. It would always be six, half past, which is quite early, but those half past four mornings they were…

Josh: What would you do?

Sue: Well, cry a lot. I'd look out of the window, see if there were any other lights on. Am I the only one up? We used to have a cup of tea and a digestive biscuit, waiting for Anne Diamond to come on at silly o'clock.

Rob: On the telly, not round for a cup of tea.

Sue: And then she'd come on looking all lovely. And there was us, with a digestive and a cup of tea, waiting for the day to begin, which was going to go on forever.

Rob: So, if I woke up at 4.30, talk us through the bedtime with the three kids. Was Joe born at that point?

Sue: Yeah. You were about two and a half, and still getting up at 4.30. But you would sleep for two hours in the day, and then you would go to bed at six. And I tried keeping you up all day, putting you to bed late, but you still got up at half past four. So, I thought might as well have the two hours in the day, and at least you went to bed at six. And I had Dan, who was at school, who was eight or nine, doing homework, football clubs. And then, when I had Joe, Joe used to wake up about two o'clock in the morning for a feed, and not settle. Then Rob would get up at half past four. I had to stop driving for a little while because I couldn't remember where I'd been because I was so tired. I used to have to

217

pick Dan up from school at 3.30. So I would leave about 12.30, put them two in a buggy, and just walk around. Because I knew they were safe, getting lots of fresh air.

Rob: What was this grinning idiot doing while I was out there?

Sue: He was at work.

Dave: No. At weekends, I used to get up too and then one of us would go back to bed again.

Sue: Yeah, we did a lot of shifts.

Josh: What job were you doing at that stage?

Dave: I think I was on Shell, driving tankers.

Sue: Petrol tankers.

Rob: He crashed one.

Josh: Did you?

Dave: Yeah. Well, not crashed it, just rolled over.

Rob: He fractured his skull, tipped it over a roundabout.

Sue: And then I had a big operation, and we had two children under four, and an older one.

Josh: Oh, wow. So how many years did that go on?

Sue: I suppose it went on until Joe went to school. Then at least I got a break during the day.

Rob: It was seven years.

Sue: Yeah, probably. It was a long slog.

Rob: It paid off though.

Sue: Yeah. Joe's lovely... No, that was a joke, Rob.

Josh: And Dave said he wasn't that fussed about having girls. Did you care if you had a girl?

Sue: When I had Dan, the eldest one, I wanted a girl, because David already had two boys. So, I thought it would be nice to have a little girl. And then I had two miscarriages. So, by the time Rob came, as long as I had a baby, I was happy. And then, by the time my Joe came along, I just thought, oh, it'd be easy, just all boys.

Dave: You were on for fertility treatment.

Sue: For five years to have Dan.

Dave: And him. It took six years, didn't it, for Rob?

Sue: So, really, I was just glad there was going to be a baby.

Rob: Basically, you thought you weren't going to have a third, let's not rubber up. And then look what happened.

Sue: Joe.

Josh: The next question is from Kirsty from Yateley. What toys did Rob like as a child?

Sue: Rob loved his farm and lining up the animals. He loved a toy called Oh Penny. And it was a little doll that had horses, didn't you?

Dave: He loved the kitchen. He had a kitchen.

Josh: So, they were quite feminine toys?

Sue: A farm's not feminine.

Rob: Yeah. I think I've got quite a feminine side.

Josh: Yeah. So he wasn't a rough-and-tumble kid then?

Sue: Well, he was when he played football.

Dave: They called him rhino. Because he just went in. He didn't see any other players. He saw the ball.

Rob: I was really weirdly committed as a kid to things, wasn't I? So, if I was doing football, I was doing it like the professionals would.

Josh: Was he good, or did he just really try hard?

Sue: Both really. You were good.

Rob: No, I was all right at football but I really got into eating pizza for each dinner. I did hunt for attention, but when I was little, how did you used to position Dan in the room, when I wasn't allowed to play with his toys?

Sue: Yes. But when you say this, you were one year old. So, you were just walking about and messing them up. So I put Dan in a corner with a pouffe in front of him so he could play quietly.

Rob: Footstool, they're called. Let's just keep it woke.

Sue: Anyway… And then Rob had the rest of the room to play.

Rob: I think it created the monster. I think it created a middle child syndrome.

Sue: You were only one, you wouldn't even remember that.

Rob: Well, I have, haven't I?

Sue: I think someone must have told you.

Rob: Talking about toys, my mum's been desperate to buy a pink baby doll, for a girl, for years. Because she had boys. And when we said we were having a girl, she was like...

Sue: I'll get the doll.

Rob: So she gave my firstborn a doll that, I would say, was three times the size of the actual baby. So, we had this big box, this big pink doll.

Sue: Beautiful.

Rob: Was it from Swanley market?

Sue: No, it was a shop... at Swanley.

Rob: It sat in our bedroom, in that tiny flat. And every time I looked at it, I was like, 'It's still bigger than my child. When is she ever going to play with it?'

Sue: She's grown into it now. Oh, I love the girls.

Josh: Your brother, has he got boys as well?

Rob: He's got a boy and a girl, and then my other, older two brothers have, well, one's got a boy and a girl. So, there's these two kids that are similar age. And my older brother Dan's not had kids yet. So it's quite good actually, because Mum and Dad aren't too overworked, babysitting-wise. You can still access them pretty well. And your knee's not too bad at the moment, is it? I'm getting Mum injections, like John Terry for the World Cup.

Sue: No. I've had the injection so I'll be all right.

Dave: She's all right to go to bingo.

Sue: I had one in this leg and I've got one in this leg the end of the month. And then I'm going to have another one in each leg when we go to Australia.

Rob: You'll be a guest on *The Last Leg* in a minute.

Josh: Are you going to Australia with Rob?

Sue: Yeah. For the tour.

Josh: Nice. You excited?

Sue: Rob is. He can't wait to take us.

Rob: I'm dropping them off at my mum's brother halfway through. Can't do a full three and a half weeks.

Josh: We'll come to Rob being a comedian, because we've got lots of questions on that. But, one more on Rob as a child: Catherine from Brisbane, Australia. What modern things would you like to have had when Rob was a baby?

Sue: Oh, that bottle warmer that you had. I love that. When we used to stay around, I thought, this is like magic.

Josh: What was it like then? What kind of stuff were you using, bottle-wise?

Sue: Boiling the kettle, making it, and then cooling it down in the middle of the night. So, I thought that warmer was amazing. That all came out the right temperature in seconds, didn't it?

Rob: Yeah. You just put a bottle in, you press how many ounces you're making, and it does the right amount of boiled water. You scoop it in, six scoops, press it again, fills it up, perfect temperature. Perfect amount.

Sue: Other than that, I think there are too many gadgets, really. I think they over-complicate babies.

Rob: I agree.

Josh: What gadgets would you get rid of?

Sue: They've got to have a thing to strengthen their neck. They've got to lie on it that way. Then, they've got something else to stretch this. They do that playing.

Rob: Tummy time. There's a write-off.

Sue: I think there are too many people making too much money.

Josh: Did you have these things? Did you have tummy time when they were kids?

Sue: No.

Dave: They used to say that, one time, the best way was on the back.

Sue: Oh, to sleep? Yeah.

Dave: Yeah. To put them to sleep, and then they changed it to on the belly.

Sue: Oh, they had to go on their side, to be put to sleep. I don't know where they go now.

Rob: I would say I agree with that, about too many gadgets, but you also were put on a watch list with the amount of accidents me and my brothers had, because we were fighting so much.

Sue: We did go to A & E quite a lot, but I thought that's just boys. We thought you ate slug pellets once. So I rang the hospital and said, 'I'm not sure, because he'd got them and put them in a watering can.' The woman on the phone was all, 'Let me just go through to the poison unit.' I said, 'Okay.' She rang me back and said, 'Can you pop him down?' So I said, 'Oh, yeah.' She said, 'Have you got a car or do you need an ambulance?' I said, 'Oh, no, I've got a car. I'll come down now.' When I got there, there were about four men all in white coats waiting for us because, apparently, if you have eaten them, you can die. Anyway, they made him sick and he hadn't eaten them.

Rob:: Once, I broke my wrist playing football, and I came home and Mum sent me to bed with two paracetamol.

Sue: And a packet of peas on your arm.

Dave: And you phoned me up at work.

Rob: I had to ring my dad at work once, where I was having an anaphylactic shock, with a severe reaction from cherries, and my mum wasn't listening to me. She just went, 'Go to bed. Go to bed.' So I had to ring my dad. And I came down the stairs, and I looked like I was about to burst, and I handed you the phone, didn't I? And what did you do after that?

Sue: The nurse around the corner came round and gave you two antihistamines, and I had to take you straight to hospital.

Rob: And did I hit my head open in France as well?

Sue: Oh, no. That was Joe. We took him to the hospital. And, in France, you had to stay there and wait for a doctor in a room. So we waited and the doctor came and stitched his head. And then, as we were leaving, we had to sign some papers and we turned around and Rob had gone. He was three, three and a half. I couldn't find him anywhere. So I said, 'Oh, let's just go down. We've got this baby with stitches in and we can't find him.' So, we got in the lift, we pressed the wrong button and went to the kitchen in the basement. We came up a floor. I said, 'Let's get Joe in the car with Dan,' because Dan was still sitting in the car.

Rob: You left Dan in the car on his own?

Sue: Yeah. He was about nine or ten.

Rob: Okay. I think we've gone over that too quickly, but fine. Nine-year-old in a car on his own.

Sue: In France. Well, I had you and the baby.

Rob: You didn't have me, you'd lost me.

Josh: At this point, how much are you panicking?

Sue: Oh, quite a lot.

Rob: She's lost two of the three – I would be too.

Sue: Wasn't a good day.

Rob: The only one's she's got is bleeding.

Sue: So, I said, 'Let's take Joe back to the car with Dan, and put him in the car and then we'll have a look.' And when we got back to the car, he's standing by the car.

Dave: He'd got back in the lift.

Sue: He got in the lift, on his own. I said to him, 'Did you go to the kitchen?' He said, 'No.'

Josh: Did you genuinely get put on a watch list?

Sue: No, no. But I used to say to him, when they started doing dangerous things, I used to say, 'Look, I'm not going to casualty today. We're not going to A & E.'

Rob: Yeah. But wasn't I with Dad when I cracked my head open?

Dave: Yeah. There were Morris dancers, and you couldn't see. So I stood you on the table, and I don't know, you must have stepped back and you'd just done your head, and I put you on my shoulders and touched your head and it was all wet. You didn't cry. So, Dan came with me, and you stayed with Joe, I think?

Sue: Yeah. I was breastfeeding Joe.

Dave: And I took him to the hospital, and I said, 'If you're a good boy, you can go to the machines and have a treat.' And he went in there and they didn't even put anaesthetic in. He just sat there.

Rob: So I had stitches without anaesthetic? I didn't know I was rock hard.

Josh: You got to watch Morris dancers, though.

Rob: Oh, I love Morris dancers.

Sue: But the funny thing was, Dave can never remember a birthday or full names or anything like that. So it

229

was a good job Dan went with him, because Dan was only about ten or 11. They said to him, 'What's his date of birth?' And he's looking at Dan.

Dave: Yeah, Dan knew.

Sue: Most people do, though.

Josh: Was Rob a confident child? Because obviously, Rob's confident in a room with people now, really good. Was he always good conversationally?

Sue: He used to chat, but he was quiet, and he was, as I say, quite sensitive. And the only time when your character really came out was when you played football. Because you were confident in what you were doing, and you loved it. So he was very definite about what he was doing. But he wasn't a loud child or anything like that. He was a very loving child. Quite sensitive, really.

Rob: Very nervous, wasn't I?

Sue: Nervous. Well, more sensitive really, I would say.

Rob: I think it's when the front teeth come out, I turned.

Josh: Did you always have big teeth?

Sue: I didn't know he had big teeth till he went on the telly and everybody said it.

Rob: We've all got the same massive mouth.

Josh: Claire from Kent asked, what's the most dangerous thing that Rob's done?

Sue: Dangerous thing? Probably something on League, is it *League of Their Own* or something? One of those dangerous things.

Josh: Did you worry about him when he went out as a teenager?

Sue: Oh, yeah. Terribly. All of them.

Rob: I didn't go out much, really. Not until I was older. I was quite a good boy.

Sue: Well, then you went to university at 18, didn't you? But I did worry. I didn't like him going out. We used to have an iron gate at the back of where we lived and you had to have a key to get in. I'd be in the back bedroom, trying to go to sleep, so when I used to hear that gate I'd think, 'They're home now. I think I'll sleep.'

Josh: And they wouldn't have had mobile phones or anything like that?

Dave: No.

Josh: And did he used to get in trouble at school or anything?

Sue: No, he didn't. It sounds like I'm bragging but the three of them, every time I went to parents' evening, I loved it. Because they just used to say nice things about my children and everybody wants to hear that.

Dave: Can I just say, I've remembered something. We sent him to the same infant school juniors as Dan, and we went to see some first report from the teacher, and she said, 'Well, what can I say about Rob? He's never going to be a high flyer.' At five years old!

Sue: She said, 'What I suggest you do is get down to the Early Learning Centre and get some flashcards.' I looked at her and I thought, *Well, he's not staying here; you've written him off at five!* So we changed schools and he flourished.

Rob: Yeah. And I stormed those Ds and Es.

Sue: You did, yeah. Didn't we all?

Josh: Ryan, from Dorset, asked, what was Rob's work ethic like as a child? Because obviously now, he's very driven, really works hard, has done really well. Could you see that in him?

Sue: Yeah, always. But Dave's a very hard worker. Dave's got a great work ethic and he gets it from Dave. If Rob had a project at school, it would always be done the best he could do. His football, everything he did.

Rob: Well, I think when Dad was working, he used to work 12-hour shifts sometimes. Especially if we had to go on holiday and he couldn't earn money because he was a cab driver. When we were away, Dad would do two weeks, 12 hours a day, longer, just until he had X amount of money. He'd basically stay in the cab until he earned X amount and would come home. So, when I started gigging, I was like, 'Well, I'm only doing 20 minutes a night. Why can't I be out of the house for 14 hours? And if I can do as many gigs as possible and I'm enjoying it.' So I just based my effort on how much Dad was working really. And Dad picked me up quite a lot actually, in the cab, when I was gigging in London.

Josh: Charge you?

Rob: No, he'd pop the meter on just so I'd know how much it would've been.

Dave: If somebody stopped me and said, 'I need to go to the airport,' I'd have chucked him out.

Rob: That was the rule. If there was someone with a suitcase, I'd have to get out. But I would've got out as well, because that's a big fare.

Josh: Did you live with your folks when you started comedy?

Rob: Yeah. So, I went to uni, to do tourism, in Canterbury, and I stayed there for a year after because I got a job. But, I quit that job to come home. And that's when I started, when I was about 23, about a year after moving home.

Josh: Well, let's go to that then. When did you find out Rob was doing stand-up? How many gigs had you done?

Sue: I don't remember how many he'd done, but we knew he was doing it in the evenings.

Dave: Yeah. Sandy saw him at the... Up the Creek, isn't it?

Josh: Was Up the Creek your first gig?

Rob: Yeah.

Josh: And how'd it go?

Rob: All I remember is, the lights being so bright and it was a... Well, it was weird though, because I'd emailed, thinking they'd never reply. But this guy who worked there, Simon, emailed back straight away, because he'd just come back from Edinburgh and he hadn't been bothered to go through all the emails. Mine was the first one. There was a waiting list of hundreds of people. But he was like, 'Yeah. If you can do it, come down Sunday.' I was like, 'Shit!' I'm confident now, but I wasn't confident then really. I was quite shy. I was waiting to pick up my brother from the station and I remember listening to The Smiths' song, 'Ask', and it says about how shyness is nice, but shyness can stop you doing things you've always wanted to do. I thought, that's a good sentiment. Because I want to do it, but I'm scared. So let's not let that get in the way. So, I went down there. And then in the interval, before I went on, that song played. And then I had two pints and went on. That's all I remember; it was so bright.

Josh: Oh, wow. And did it go well?

Rob: Yeah. For a first gig, it was fine. I went on, said a few funny things.

Josh: Did you know anyone there? Did you invite your brothers or anything?

Rob: No one. I didn't invite anyone for years.

Josh: And do you remember the first time you saw Rob?

Sue: Would it have been Leicester Square?

Rob: I think it might be Leicester Square, New Comedian of the Year competition, because I got to the final, and it was quite a big deal.

Josh: Rob put on a Facebook group that he couldn't do a gig because he was now too much of a big shot, because he'd won Leicester Square, Comedian of the Year.

Rob: That is actual bollocks. I've never used the term big shot in my entire—

Josh: I'm paraphrasing.

Rob: I've thought it. I wouldn't say it out loud.

Josh: Were you nervous the first time you saw him?

Sue: Yeah, terribly.

Rob: I remember when I did a gig, Just the Tonic, in that same room, that you came and watched, because Dad was driving me home afterwards. You went, 'Do you want a drink?' I was like, 'No.' And then, just before I went on, you held my hand.

Sue: Yeah, I was really nervous the first time I saw him do it, but then he just looked so confident and I just thought, nobody dies from a bad joke.

Josh: Was he a different person on stage to the person you knew?

Sue: He seemed to shine when he was on there, like that's where he should be. It looked like he was comfortable.

Rob: Mum and Dad come and see me so much. You've seen me about eight, ten times on this tour. They just go around the country on the piss-up with all their mates. So, they'll be in Wigan, they'll be in Newcastle, Liverpool. They've got mates everywhere.

Sue: Devon.

Rob: Devon. Oh, yeah, because they came up to Liverpool and they booked the train that takes about nine hours or something, stopping at every station.

Sue: I was trying to book a seat on it and they said you can't book a seat on there. That's strange, isn't it? Can't book a seat? And then we got on it, and then you couldn't even get a cup of coffee on it.

Josh: When did you realise that Rob was famous? Do you remember that?

Sue: Not really. I think we've been a bit... I just think we know him, and he's good, and he's on the telly.

But I think when you did the Palladium, when
you hosted it.

Rob: Oh, with the Royal Variety?

Sue: Yeah, I was so proud. And to host that, we watched
that as kids. My dad loved it. He loved Jimmy Tarbuck,
and all those acts on there, and Tommy Cooper. So,
that was a big night in our house. We'd have snacks
and it was quite a big thing. So when he hosted it,
I was like, wow, that's Rob. He's doing that.

Dave: When we realised he was well known was when we'd
go out with him and then somebody would come up
and say, 'Oh, can I have a photo?'

Josh: Do you like it? Do you enjoy that?

Sue: No.

Josh: Sean Jowett, from Canberra, Australia has asked, who
do you tell that Rob is your son?

Sue: Well, I told the physiotherapist this morning.

Dave: Oh, she tells everybody.

Sue: But he told me about his children. One's a doctor,
one's a lawyer. So he was having a nice chat, it was
just conversation.

Rob: Good for the physio.

Sue: Yeah. Oh, he's got four. They're all doing
             marvellously.

Josh: So how do you say it? You say, 'Do you know who
             my son is?'

Sue: No, I don't say that. And I don't tell anybody if I'm
             trying to buy something because they think we're
             rich. So I don't mention it. And if they ask me, I
             don't acknowledge you. And when we've agreed a
             price, then I say, he's my son, so I get good service.

Rob: The amount of people that come to my shows on
             guest tickets. One's a baker, for Mum to get a free
             loaf of bread. You came with a seamstress the
             other week.

Dave: Yeah, but she takes all my stuff up.

Josh: So, do you watch everything he does on TV?

Sue: Yeah. We've stopped Sky Plussing it all now because
             it was full up, because he got that famous.

Josh: You're over-exposed, mate. Filled up Sky Plus.

Rob: Yeah. Their hard drive's full.

Sue: We just do selective bits now.

Rob: I'm going to get them an external hard drive for Christmas.

Sue: *Taskmaster*. I loved him on that. That was so funny. And *Rob and Romesh*, that's good, isn't it?

Josh: This is a question I'm really excited about. It's from Letitia, from Barcelona, Spain. What are your thoughts on Rob's parenting?

Sue: I think he's a brilliant parent.

Dave: Yeah, he's a very good dad.

Josh: Is he how you'd imagine him as a dad?

Sue: Better. And Dan, our other son, they're both really good dads. Really good. They're hands on, they're firm when they need to be, but they're fun. They're understanding with them. Yeah, I'm really impressed. Really good dad.

Josh: Were you surprised when he told you he was going to become a dad? Did you always imagine him being a dad?

Sue: Yeah. I just thought they would all have children. I suppose because that's what I did.

Josh: And is he a different parent to you? Can you tell the difference in the generations?

Sue: Not really.

Rob: I was a bit nervous at the start. I imagine you probably were, and I didn't see that, but I think everyone's a bit nervous at the beginning.

Dave: Yeah. With the first baby you used to both change her at the same time.

Josh: And what's it like being grandparents?

Sue: Oh, lovely. I love it. Absolutely love it.

Josh: You're really hands-on grandparents.

Dave: Yeah. We have them overnight, maybe for a couple of days if necessary.

Josh: How do you get on with the early mornings, though?

Sue: Well, we tend to live like students, to be honest. There's no routine. We keep saying, we're going to go to bed early. We manage to get up about 12, don't we? But Friday night, we had friends come down. At a quarter to one Saturday morning, we were still singing in the garden because we had lunch and drinks and the neighbours came back and they came in. We used the new speaker. So, we were doing requests with the new speaker.

Josh: And then you have to look after your grandchildren, and your life changes.

Sue: Yeah. I'll say to the children, 'You need to practise getting up later.' And they say to me, 'You need to practise getting up earlier.' But they come in about half past five, full of the joys of spring.

Rob: Normally, we try to hold them back and let them in about seven, which is still too early for you. But if we're not here, then you're just up at half five. So, if I'm away working or something, and they've had them up since half five and it's a weekend, they've been with them the whole time. I come home about two o'clock and they both look like they're about to die. Like they've aged 15 years. They're limping along, Mum's upstairs passed out. He heaves himself around, trying to make a cup of tea.

But that's the only thing that you struggle with, is that early start. Everything else you don't... When they were younger, it was nappies. We're really lucky, me and Lou, to have you two and her parents so close because it makes such a massive difference.

Josh: So, in your busy schedule of getting up at 2pm and stuff, do you listen to the podcast?

Dave: Yeah.

Josh: Have you listened to all of them?

Sue: No, I'm saving some of them for when we go to Spain.

Josh: Do you enjoy it?

Dave: Yeah, love it. It's very funny.

Sue: I love all the different guests and listening to different people's parenting. Because you think everybody's going to do it the same and they don't.

Rob: Do you think it's a fair reflection of what's going on in my house with the kids?

Sue: Definitely.

Rob: Even though we're older now, you still find it interesting, even though you haven't got young kids?

Sue: Oh, yeah. I love children anyway. And it's just, I like to hear about what they think is the right thing to do, bringing up children. You can't have one rule for every child. I had three children and they all slept differently. When I had my first child, I thought I was just a wonderful mother. I had the other two, then realised no, I was just lucky.

Rob: That's the problem. Dan was a bit of a golden boy because he was perfect, slept non-stop, whenever you wanted him to sleep.

Sue: Brought him home from the hospital, first night, slept through. Honestly.

Dave: Eleven o'clock, he went to sleep. We fed him and I think he woke up about seven in the morning or something like that.

Dave: He didn't even cry, did he?

Rob: And it was like that for six years, and I came along.

Josh: Oh my word! So, when Rob came along, you couldn't believe it happened?

Sue: No, I thought I was doing it wrong now. I thought God gave me the wrong child, or I've lost my skills. I was in a little waiting room when I was in labour with Rob, and the midwife said, 'I've got to go, it's half past four. You're not going to have this baby till 10 o'clock tonight. I would wait, but I've got the builders coming in.' So she went home and a new midwife came in. I said, 'I'm having this baby, the baby's coming.' And nobody believed me. Dad said, 'No, the woman said you're not having it till ten.' He went out and got a nurse and you were born in the side room.

So that's why on that baby picture of you, you're wrapped in a green gown. There was no cot or anything in this room.

Josh: In those days, what was the role of the father in the birth?

Dave: Oh, I was there.

Josh: Was that a debate in those days?

Dave: No. Years ago when I had my first two sons, you weren't allowed; they just sent you home.

Rob: My other brother, Russ, was born New Year's Eve. So were you at a party?

Dave: Well, I was in the pub. They said, 'Off you go and we'll let you know when the baby's here.' You weren't allowed even near it. But Dan was the first one, then you and I just loved it. It was lovely to see and holding them straight away.

Josh: Do you give Rob parenting tips? Is it difficult? Because I always think that's one of the things grandparents say is – they find it difficult to sit back if they feel like...

Sue: Well, I think he's a really good parent. If he was doing something that I thought was really wrong,

I'd say, are you sure you should be doing that? Or have you tried this?

Josh: Does he come to you for advice?

Sue: I don't know if he needs it really.

Dave: Sometimes I think, especially when they were younger.

Sue: The only time I would intervene would be if I thought the children were in danger or neglected or not being looked after.

Rob: If they kept on falling off tables in pubs, getting lost in France, left in the car. Stuff like that. Nothing major.

Sue: You learn from your mistakes.

Entertaining
Your Child

'Once, I looked round [the cinema] and saw about nine sleeping mums and dads, with their little kids staring forward, off their tits on sugar.'

Rob: It never stops. From 6am when they wake up until whenever they pass out and finally go to sleep. You can't tire them out, they will keep going and going and going. The only way to calm them down is make them bored. If you keep finding new activities it just jazzes them up more and more. I used to put them in the car and do a loop around the M25 because at worst they are strapped in and not moving and at best asleep in silence. Obviously I can't do that now because the price of petrol makes a lap of the M25 as expensive as a weekend in Legoland.

Josh: Can we start by taking a moment to discuss just how stressful the play park is? Before I had kids, I presumed the park to be a magical land where you would sit on a bench in the afternoon sun and sip a latte while watching your cherished offspring laughing with new friends, high on sugar and see-saws. Perhaps you would take a photo of your child playing that you would hashtag #toosweet on Instagram. Perhaps you would fall into chat with another parent, exchange witticisms about how parenting is tough but it is moments like this that make it worth it.

I recognise none of these things from my life.

It will surprise no one reading this that I never enjoyed playing outside as a child. Due to the lack of other children in my village I would spend my summers playing with Adam and Christopher Campkin, two brothers who made Bear Grylls feel like Lorraine Kelly. They would climb trees, ride bikes and swim in lakes – because living in Devon in the 1990s was like being in *The Railway Children*. I didn't do any of these things; I was too scared to climb trees, wasn't buoyant enough to swim in a lake and considered the removal of stabilisers from my bike to be a needless risk. My main experience of the park growing up was Adam and Christopher's parents taking us to the slides – not the normal ones but a particular 1990s phenomenon: death slides. A slide that just fell vertically and almost certainly has now been banned under health and safety standards. Adam and Christopher loved these slides, I would just stand at the side and watch, being the kind of square that didn't see death as a selling point. It is a huge injustice that someone so cautious should be the one to end up with a bad neck.

Consequently, there is an argument that my issue with parks is that I am projecting my own anxieties on to my daughter. Because for me, taking a child to the park is being in a constant state of fear that my daughter is about to die on a see-saw. It's okay for Rob, he's the kind of chilled-out guy who can watch his daughter climb a ladder without thinking, 'What if she suddenly decides to let go and falls two feet?' I'm not that guy. I'm the guy hovering behind his daughter, cramping her style and getting shakes of the head from other, cooler/less caring parents.

And the stress doesn't stop there. Then you have the other children. The worst type of children, ones that aren't yours. Children that walk up the slides, spin smaller children too fast on roundabouts and constantly push in the queue in front of your own child (something I of course allow as I am apparently scared of an eight-year-old). At the weekend, our local park becomes feral, like a post-apocalyptic movie in which there is only one slide left on Earth and every remaining child on the planet is fighting to the death to use it. (Note to self: remember to pitch this idea to my agent.)

But still my daughter wants to go to the park and, more importantly, never wants to leave, because here is something no child has ever said in the park: 'I think I'm just about done, shall we go home?' This is mainly because the park has no end, it just remains the same; they can go round and round and round forever. Meals end, journeys end, *Peppa Pig* ends, parks are infinite. The only way out of a park is to tell your child that if you leave you will buy them an ice cream. Bribery, always a sign you are nailing parenting.

Worst of all are the parks they have put in other tourist attractions, meaning you can travel for hours, pay to go somewhere and still find yourself back in the park. I've been in parks in London Zoo, on the South Bank and on a Greek beach. When we took our daughter to a safari park in Kent (no, really), did she want to see the rhino or the giraffe? No, she wanted to go on a swing exactly like the one 100 yards from our door. It is very difficult to explain to a three-year-old how much more exciting it is for an elephant to be in Kent than a slide; once you start using the words 'natural habitat' you know you have lost the battle. When you start discussing the cost of petrol and the price of tickets, you are actively damaging your relationship with your offspring.

Rob: I got mine into the cinema at an early age as that meant I could get some sleep while they watched the film. I would get them sweets and popcorn and I would sit in the middle of them with my arms on their laps holding their hands. I would then fall asleep within the first five minutes and then wake up for the finale of the film. The only reason I would wake up would be due to the loud noises that normally erupt when a kids' film is building to its crescendo. As the baddie took the one final blow to the face after a big explosion, I would be jerked awake in panic, popcorn flying everywhere. I would hurriedly look to my right and left and hope my children were still there. It's a lot easier now they are older as I'm not as scared of them running away or being kidnapped so I can sleep a bit more peacefully. Don't judge me, there are loads of parents asleep in there. Once, I looked round and saw about nine sleeping mums and dads, with their little kids staring forward, off their tits on sugar.

I've never seen the middle of any children's film. Whether I'm at home on the sofa or in a cinema, I will fall asleep, that is a 100 per cent guarantee. I can tell you everything you need to know about the start of kids' movies but nothing thereafter. I think my *Mastermind* specialist subject would be the first five minutes of every kids' film made since the birth of my first child. The falling asleep is starting to get out of hand, though. I fell asleep as the lights went down before the start of the West End show *The Lion King* – it was so cosy and dark. However, I had the shock of my life when I heard the infamous 'Ah Zabenya' opening lyric. I nearly jumped out of my skin after hearing that being belted out during my deep slumber.

Josh: One of the areas I am certain that Rob will be better as a parent than me is in playing. Here is a man who doesn't question himself or feel self-conscious. He'd be quite happy to pretend to be a shopkeeper without thinking, *Oh God, am I sounding like a bit of a knob?* I try but I am just too uptight to pretend I am a dinosaur without thinking, what if someone sees? I am not good at impressions. I make up for this lack of commitment to the role of diplodocus by buying my daughter too many toys. The toys that she really wants more than any others are the worst toys of all: plastic shit on the front of magazines. You will go into the newsagent to buy a bag of Popchips and suddenly there is no way of leaving without a spin-off magazine for a Nickelodeon show about a talking mongoose she hasn't even seen and quite frankly I am not sure even exists. They could put a pink jewellery box on the front of *The New Statesman* and my daughter would want to buy it.

Rob: It is true that I love silly games. When we are at home, I am pretty good at thinking about ways to entertain the kids. One of my favourite games is 'TRAP'. This is where I lie on their bedroom floor face down. The bed is their safe base where I can't get them, but when they are off the bed I can trap them with my arms and legs as they scream and squeal trying to wriggle out. It's absolutely joyous but normally ends up with them sweaty, blood red and injured. But that's the price of fun! I've got to be honest though and say I don't really need to entertain my kids any more. When we just had our eldest it was full-on playing and the park and activities. But now they play so well together I actually get told to leave their bedroom as it's not a game for grown-ups. Of course I take them out and we do things as a family indoors but it feels so natural, like we are hanging out as mates. If they get bored, I just enforce the classic toy shop/McDonald's drive thru double. It's always a winner.

Josh: The first Christmas when my daughter was old enough to know what was going on we went too hard with the presents, not realising she had no idea how many she was meant to get and would have been happy with one, not 23. At the end of the festive season, we were left with a pile of toys our daughter never wanted but would now never forgive us for getting rid of. On top of this we had set an insanely high bar for the following years that has now ruined our lives. The only thing that cheered me up about the situation was going for a walk on Boxing Day past our local Oxfam and seeing a toy drum kit and keyboard dumped outside. However badly our Christmas presents had gone, it didn't compare to the story of that family and that toy.

Rob: My kids almost definitely watch too many films and TV shows, but it's how I make a living, so it seems mad to complain. In order to get them off the screens, Lou does an activity big shop every couple of months either online or at The Works/Hobbycraft, where we will get sticker books, colouring in, painting and an assortment of activity books. Then we put them in a big box and let them pick something out as a bribe when we are trying to get them off the TV or screen. I don't know why but kids love picking something out of a box – they get so excited. I think we still like it as adults to be honest. *Deal or No Deal* was mega popular and it was just opening boxes. We even put up with Noel Edmonds just so we could see some boxes open and close.

Josh: If you weren't surprised that I hated playing outside as a child, then prepare to be equally underwhelmed by the news that I spent a lot of my childhood watching television. (Why not read my book about it, *Watching Neighbours Twice a Day*, available in all good bookshops!) Thirty years on, this love of children's TV hasn't left me, and I adore CBeebies. Worryingly, perhaps more than my daughter does. Such is my love for *JoJo & Gran Gran, Grace's Amazing Machines, Moon and Me, Something Special* and every show except *In the Night Garden* that sometimes when my daughter has gone to bed but left the TV on I won't turn it over from CBeebies straight away. Instead I will find myself – an adult male of 39 – sucked into an episode of *Waffle the Wonder Dog*, thinking I can't carry on my evening without finding out if Waffle gets paint everywhere as they try to decorate this room (answer: yes).

I will admit these actions make me sound at best sad and at worst creepy. But I know I'm not alone because I now find myself discussing these shows with other parents, debating with adults in their late thirties who is funnier out of the bag from *Sarah & Duck* or the crabs from *Hey Duggee*, while offering up my opinion that Mr Tumble is the greatest comic performer on UK television (except Romesh, obviously). Part of the reason we are doing this is it makes us feel part of an exclusive club, quite a strange club where the cost of membership is being able to name all five squirrels in *Hey Duggee*. While our friends without children can talk about how they were out last night till 3am, they don't even know which one is Charlie and which one is Lola, so who are the losers? (Answer: us.)

When I was a kid, television was the bad guy. Watch too much and you would destroy your mind, sit too close and you would destroy your eyes. I know some people don't like their kids watching TV but I'm fine with it – you've got to give yourself a break sometime. In fact, TV is now educational; someone told me recently that if you put subtitles on then it helps your child's literacy by 40 per cent. I have absolutely no idea what that really means and haven't googled it in case it is wrong, but I am hanging on to that fact as proof I'm a good parent. Popping on the subtitles and telling myself I'm not just putting my daughter in front of *Bing*, I'm starting her on the long road to studying English at Oxford.

Going to School or Nursery

'We recently got an email warning about scarlet fever. I hadn't previously worried about my daughter getting that as I am not bringing her up in medieval times.'

Josh: And then, after being in the house with this tiny screaming human being for what seems like forever, you decide that you are going to hand them over to a more responsible adult. I have heard talk of some parents worrying about leaving their children at nursery for the first time, struggling to put trust in people to look after their precious offspring. This makes me feel slightly guilty as, full disclosure, this didn't even enter my mind. My theory was that I have no idea what I am doing as a parent and I got away with it so surely a trained professional will be fine.

The only worry I have about the carers at my daughter's nursery is that they tend to do too good a job, which makes me look bad. I will ask my daughter what she has been up to with her day and she will say they went to the park, learned about the life cycle of creepy crawlies before making a collage of a hedgehog from twigs and autumn leaves, and I will think, well, if you enjoyed that then your weekend of playing games on the CBeebies app so I can have a lie-in is going to be slightly

257

underwhelming. Just once I want to pick her up and hear that they just watched *Topsy and Tim* while her key carer looked at the Plymouth Argyle message boards on her iPhone. Other parents may say that isn't what we pay for, but I would say it keeps expectations comfortably low.

It won't surprise you that my daughter goes to a very East London nursery. To give you an idea of it, in her class there are three different boys called Jago. If that doesn't create a vivid enough image, let me tell you that I was once waiting for my daughter when I saw a man with a man bun waiting to pick up his son and when his son appeared, he also had a man bun. The child was three, social services should have been called.

Rob: Without schools looking after and teaching your children for seven hours a day, your life would be a living hell. Don't get me wrong, I love my children more than anything in this world, but you can't function properly in each other's company 24 hours a day, seven days a week. I think we all learnt that during the lockie Ds. I don't even think schools exist for educational purposes – they're just an excuse for parents to have a break. It's the same with my visits to the rubbish dump. I don't need to go down there as regularly as I do. In reality I need to go once a month, but I like a weekly visit for a bit of alone time. My local dump has a CCTV camera you can view on the council website to see how busy it is. I like to check the camera to make sure that when I visit it's the busiest time with the longest queue. That way I get to sit in the traffic listening to a podcast. The disposal of some boxes isn't the main motivation – I'm attracted to the peace and quiet of my local landfill site.

The purpose of schools is so that parents don't lose their

marbles. Just thinking about home schooling in lockdown makes me shudder. Some people enjoy home schooling and choose to do it outside of once-in-a-century pandemics. They make a conscious decision to educate and teach their own children in their own home full-time. You know what, good for them – we are all different and shouldn't be judged. In the same way some people like to go to sex clubs in Berlin to be pissed and shat on while being beaten with a paddle and having 'you worthless dirty maggot' shouted at them over and over again as a second person stamps on their bollocks in work boots. We are all different. Who am I to judge?

Josh: There is no silence as shocking as your house the first time you return from dropping your child at nursery. Is this what the house used to be like? Did it used to echo like a haunted castle in *Scooby-Doo*? Did I always own a grandfather clock? Then you realise, this is the moment you dreamed of: your own life back how it was. Pure freedom. And then you sit down on the sofa and turn on *Homes Under the Hammer* and wonder if this is really what you have been waiting for for the last year. And then you start to miss your child.

Rob: My kids starting school was the crunch moment for me to lose some weight and get fit. We all put on some pounds when the kids are young. Mums are recovering from pregnancy and labour, and, along with that, both parents are eating a lot of quick and easy takeaways after a busy day parenting and drinking copious amounts of beer and wine to deal with the pressure of zero sleep and a million responsibilities. So now your kids are in school you finally have that free time that you longed for in order to exercise. I had so many grand plans for how sexy and unrelatably shredded I was going to get. Needless to say, it didn't happen. What happens a lot is that I come home from the school run, sit down on the sofa for 30 seconds and fall back to sleep again. Only to wake up in shock and panic late for work or the school pick-up.

Josh: To be honest, nursery isn't that tough for a parent – it's just a lovely warm-up for the actual challenge of school. I complain about the nursery run and how stressful it is but I have a 90-minute window for her to arrive and still make it for breakfast. Next year, when I have to get her in for 9am or else, I'm in the shit. I simply do not understand how people pull this off. Rob does this every day and yet when I speak to him, he doesn't sound like he has had a mental breakdown. He is just grumbling because of some rule about him not taking a dog. It is hard to think that I will look back on this period of being so late every morning that I have to get a black cab or my daughter will go hungry as the least stressful bit of my decade.

Compared to people with kids at school I have it easy. No deadlines, homework, parents' evenings, spelling tests, dreadful school plays you have to pretend you enjoy. I drop my daughter off at nursery and pick her up and ask her what she did with her day (answer: play), that's it. The fact she is alive is really 99 per cent of the battle. Because it is easier to get information out of a mafia suspect than it is to get my daughter to tell me what she did with her day.

The main way I keep in touch with what she is up to at nursery is via an online service called Tapestry, where the nursery upload pictures of the class and a small description of what they did written in Comic Sans in an attempt to trick us into thinking our children wrote it themselves. This was great in the first few years when my daughter was in a small class and I knew all the children in there. I would look at the photos and see what they were up to and which of her friends was currently on the shit list. But now she has moved into a bigger class full of kids I don't know and suddenly looking at Tapestry is quite a creepy experience for me. A way to begin my evening by sitting at my computer looking at photos of four-year-olds I don't know and reading about what they are up to. Between us I have had to stop reading for fear I will be added to some kind of list.

Rob: The pre-school morning routine and school run are pound for pound some of the most intense parenting that you can do. The Roy Jones Jr of parenting – sure, it's only an hour or so, but the stakes are dangerously high. You have to feed them, dress them, make sure they are clean, make their lunch, brush their teeth, pack their bags, brush and tie up their hair, sun cream on in the summer and hat packed. With an 8am departure looming it can get stressful as early in the morning the only thing children want to do is watch cartoons in their pyjamas.

Then there are all the extra curve balls, like World Book Day, sports day, Nativity play dress rehearsals, wear stripy tights cos it's world stripy clothes day or some bullshit. It's unrelenting. 'Daddy, I need a pound as it's wear a hat day for some charity. If I don't have a pound, I can't wear my hat.' Of course I don't have a £1 coin. No one has a £1 coin. No one has cash any more. Buses in London stopped taking cash in

July 2014. Only charity fundraising schoolchildren and trolleys need £1 coins. But now I'm a bad parent because I haven't got a quid to give my daughter for some fucking hat party I forgot about. Yes, I was emailed about it but I currently receive 15 emails a day from school that I immediately delete. I'm quite busy doing my actual job so it's hard to take on an unpaid role as my daughter's personal assistant as a side hustle.

Josh: What you don't realise before you send your child to nursery is that they are going to be exposed to other children's germs. More importantly, they are going to take these germs and be ill for the next year of their lives. I don't remember the last time my daughter didn't have a runny nose. You think when they go to nursery that will mean you will see less of them but you are wrong – they will still be at home but now they will be ill, and you will be paying nursery for the privilege. And not just normal illnesses; my daughter got something called hand, foot and mouth – wasn't that the thing that killed all those cows 20 years ago? We recently got an email warning about scarlet fever. I hadn't previously worried about my daughter getting that as I am not bringing her up in medieval times.

This is why the worst thing that can happen to your day is to see the name of the nursery appear as the caller on your phone. Suddenly your whole day collapses. It is hugely unlikely they are calling you to say that your daughter has just made a really good collage. Before you know it, your working day is over and you are off to pick up a child who has somehow got the plague. The worst thing about seeing the nursery pop up on your phone is the hope, because you know that maybe, just maybe it'll be one of those calls where they aren't telling you that your daughter has typhoid and instead they will say they are calling to ask if they can give her Calpol. 'Of course you can, mate, we are doing it all the time. If anything, I imagine she needs it due to withdrawal symptoms.' Who is saying no to that? 'I'd rather you didn't give her Calpol. I'll just take the day off work and come and get her.'

Rob: The email from school situation is an absolute joke. What happened before emails? There is no way on earth they would send all this correspondence out by post as it would cost them millions. I got an email recently titled 'Lollipop Man'. The message read:

Dear Parents,
Due to unforeseen circumstances, we will not have a lollipop man outside preschool today.

Apologies for any inconvenience caused.

Kind Regards

Grange Hill

Why the fuck do I need to know this? Why does anyone need to know this? Who cares? I like the lollipop man but I don't need an emailed correspondence on his whereabouts. I would have found out there was no lollipop man on the way to school anyway. There is no need for the heads-up. What do they think I am going to do with this information? Refuse to bring my child into school? Well, if there is no lollipop man then it looks like it's a day off today, kids. Yep, let's turn back, there's no way I'm taking a chance on that road alone. Let's head back home across the seven roads we've already conquered alone. There's no way a fully grown adult like myself could walk my child into school without a lollipop man.

Or maybe they still want my children to come into school but the email is a prompt for me to source my own lollipop man for the morning? Is it a 'Bring Your Own Lollipop Man' charity day? For one single pound coin you can bring your own lollipop man into school. It'll be me creeping around the local sheltered accommodation retirement home like a human trafficker looking for someone bored and available between 7am and 9am and 2pm and 4pm. They need to be strong enough to hold a giant lollipop, wear hi vis and deal with unpredictable British weather conditions.

Don't get me wrong, I have no issue with lollipop men or lollipop women. The lollipop man at my daughter's nursery is an absolute legend and the kids love him. Plus I must admit, in those few unforeseen circumstances, that without him, the traffic builds up and gets gridlocked. So I'm not disputing the need for the lollipoppers, but if we can't have one, then have some faith that we will cope as parents. Lollipop people, as I think we call them now in 2022, are really useful and make the school run much safer for all the parents and kids. However, if they are unavailable for a circumstance 'unforeseen' or even for that matter 'foreseen', I will be able to manage discovering the missing lollipop person information in that moment. I do not need a 24-hour notice period to psychologically prepare to cross a road alone without the assistance of a person in a bright yellow coat holding a seven-foot lollipop.

Friendship

'A six-year-old's diary is rammed... It's not like having
a child – it's like being the campaign manager of an
American politician running for president.'

Rob: In an ideal world, your kids wouldn't have any friends. They would just be your little mates forever and you wouldn't have to deal with extra snotty-nosed kids in your house.

I used to like other people's kids when I was younger before I became a dad. When I worked at Sainsbury's I would be the kind of cashier that would swipe their own nectar card to steal points as well as pulling silly faces and trying to make babies and kids laugh as they passed through my till strapped into trolleys. Now I have my own kids I couldn't give less of a shit. Maybe it's because I'm in the eye of the storm with young kids that are so time-demanding. Potentially, over time, when my kids have grown up and moved out, I will once again become broody and interested in young kids. (It's very hard to type 'be interested in young kids' without sounding like a massive paedo. The truth is I couldn't be further away from being a paedophile. Which is also exactly the kind of thing an actual paedophile would say. I'm sorry, I'm becoming far too bogged down with this nonce chat for what is supposed to be a light-hearted family read.)

Back on topic, my point is at this moment in time I haven't got the energy to care or even pretend to care about other people's children. I don't want to be shown a photo of your new baby, I'd rather have a glance at a pic of your post coffee morning shit. New babies aren't cute to me at the moment – I don't see a cute baby, I see a human that in 18 years is going to be just another person squashed into my face and space on a packed train at rush hour.

Josh: My daughter is four and her life is already like *Mean Girls*. The friendships she has with her three best friends at nursery are already more intense, rocky and meaningful than every relationship I had until I met my wife (which is, to be clear, not rocky at the time of writing). These four-year-old girls may have come together over a shared love of unicorns and rainbows, but now they are an unbreakable gang, all with their own characters, roles and deep-seated issues with each other – like a girl band on their final album before they split up and head towards inevitably disappointing solo careers.

Each day my daughter will come home and update us on which of the girls is currently her best friend and which one has been thrown out of the group – usually for the crime of having the wrong favourite colour. To us, the ups and downs of the friendships feel brutal, but to her they seem relatively mundane. 'I don't like Penny any more as she told me my favourite colour is violet,' she will say in an offhand way, a comment I will then think about until 2am. Tossing and turning while worrying my daughter will forever have no friends because she has a frankly pretentious favourite colour (I know I couldn't be friends with someone whose favourite colour is violet). The next day, they will greet each other in the morning like the favourite colour comment never even happened and I will think, *Are you guys dead inside?* I am not cut out for the hard life of being four.

Because I am emotionally unstable about these things, I feel an incredible sadness that these girls won't be friends forever. On my daughter's birthday I took a photo of her with her three best friends outside the front of my house and imagined taking a photo of them together again as teenagers in the same place. I know this won't happen because no one is still friends with the people they hung out with at nursery. At least that is what I thought until I said this to Rose and she said she has known her two best friends since the age of two. I didn't want to say it to her, but I think we can all agree this is at best a bit weird. Like those strange people you meet who are married to their first girlfriend. Show some bloody ambition!

I have a terrible feeling I am more invested in my daughter's friendships than she is. Due to us living a bit further away, she is going to a different school to her nursery friends, something she is totally fine with but I can't think about as it makes me too sad. I recently found myself suggesting to Rose that we move house so that our daughter can go to the same school as her friends, before coming to my senses and realising that is the shittest idea in history. There are many reasons to move house, but no one has ever done it to preserve a friendship between three-year-olds whose main common ground is that they like *Moana*. Stamp duty is hard enough to justify at the best of times.

Perhaps the reason I didn't realise that friendship at such a young age was so brutal was that I went to a primary school that was so small I had four children in my year. Of these there was only one other boy so he was my best friend by default (no self-respecting seven-year-old boy would be friends with a girl). Unlike my daughter and her friends, we never fell out, mainly because if we did, there was no one else to be friends with; you had no fallback position. I didn't realise until I was 11 that some people had options of who to be friends with; that you could gravitate towards people who were like you. I presumed you just had to be friends with the only other boy born in 1983 in the TQ13 postal district and then just accept that neither of you liked any of the same things. In the same way I am currently stuck being friends with Rob.

Rob: Friend is a strong word for a man you speak to on Zoom once a week. You would speak to a parole officer more often if you'd just left prison. Now the dream scenario is that your best mate has a kid at the same time as you and they play perfectly together, which means you get to hang out with your best mate forever. That almost never happens. What normally happens is if your child likes another kid and wants to be friends, it's an almost dead cert that you will have nothing in common with the parents. Or the alternative is you love the other parents, you are getting on like a house on fire and your kid comes up to you and says, 'Can we go home now? The other kid is weird. He keeps killing ants and pulling down his trousers then putting them up his bum.'

So as a parent you slowly accept your fate with these new people in your life that you don't really like and have nothing in common with. But you are doing it for the good of your child who has for some inexplicable reason formed a strong bond with their snotty-nosed gremlin. Your new parent friends don't like football, reality TV or slagging off the other school parents.

They are the worst kind of people: they are good people. They are nice people. I know that we are told being good and nice are positive traits. Which is true, but they are also boring traits.

Don't get me wrong, I'm not a nasty person junkie. I'm not trying to track down Idi Amin's youngest kid for a play date and trip to Maccy Ds for a Happy Meal. But I think you need something that winds you up or gets you going. My favourite text message to receive from someone is 'I tell you who's a wanker...' My face instantly lights up. Lou even knows what's happening from the look on my face. It's unbridled joy. She will see me smile and say, 'Oooh, who's being a wanker? Spill the beans.' If I could bottle that surge of energy and excitement my body feels when I open that message to sell, I would be an instant billionaire. First of all, you get the person's name, then you get the story why and more often than not you have a similar story about that person.

However, this is about your children making friends, not Lou and I making friends. So you make an effort for your child. They come first, you may even book a holiday or weekend away with the new parent friends and their kid for the good of your child and their new friendship group. It's not ideal but it will be fine – they are good, nice people. Then out of nowhere your child comes home from school or nursery and says, 'I don't like (insert name), they aren't my best friend any more.' All I'm thinking is, *Well, you'd better become best friends again because we are booked in for five nights in the Lake District with these boring, polite fuckers.*

Josh: I had never heard of play dates until two years ago but now my diary consists almost entirely of them. I have more play dates in one weekend than I had actual dates in my whole life as a teenager. Although this may be more of a reflection on quite what a dry spell my teenage years were. Play dates are lovely for the children but essentially a blind date for the parents, trying to build friendship when the only thing that you have in common is that you had sex at around the same time in around the same place. Although obviously it would be weird to bring this up (that's more of a second play date topic).

Play dates have been one of the main successes of my life as a parent. As much as Rob doesn't believe me, I actually really like the parents of my daughter's friends. In fact, I'm going to say it, they are now my actual friends. Guys, we have a WhatsApp group in which we exchange funny memes. I like these people so much I invited them not just to my daughter's birthday but to my own birthday (partly so that their children could hangout with my daughter so I didn't have to look after her and could have a drink, but let's not focus on that). This has led to a problem: I am now overly invested in my daughter maintaining her friendship group as I want to keep meeting up with the parents. What if my daughter falls out with them? Can I still meet up with the parents? Is that weird? Am I going to be sneaking out of the house behind my daughter's back to meet her old friends' parents for coffee, like a man having a very pedestrian affair?

Then there are the other types of play date, ones based on the parents being friends and trying to get their kids to play with each other. These are as a rule an absolute write-off, four adults awkwardly chatting while two children who have never met scream at each other over which of them gets to play with some Magna-Tiles. After about 45 minutes the first parent to crack will make some comment about their child being tired and the whole thing will be called off there and then. The next time you see the other parents you will say, 'That was lovely, we have to do that again sometime' and both think to yourselves, *we must never do that again sometime.* Of course this is the case. Think back to when you were a child and your parents made you play with their friends' kid – you would hate it. Every child of your parents' friends was weird and creepy, and the worst thing was they thought you were the weird one.

Rob: When you have two kids at primary school age, there is at least one birthday party every weekend. Sometimes two or three, and it's impossible to keep on top of it. I'm 36 and I get invited to a birthday party once every three to four years. It's normally something depressing like, 'Now the divorce has finally gone through and I've shaken off the old ball and chain, who fancies Las Vegas for nine nights? Be great to have you there to celebrate my big 43rd in style (smiley winky face with tongue out emoji).' A six-year-old's diary is rammed, making the logistics on a Saturday stupidly complicated. It's not like having a child – it's like being the campaign manager of an American politician running for president:

- Five am wake, breakfast, iPad, begrudgingly walk dog.
- Ten-minute drive to gymnastics for weekly class.
- Thirty-minute drive to trampoline park for birthday party, lunch in transit (jam sandwich thrown from front of car to the back seat).
- Forty-minute drive to paint-your-own-pottery birthday party.

- Thirty-minute drive to church hall for ear-splittingly loud disco party. Hopefully feed child there. Child obviously didn't eat anything apart from sugar.
- Twenty-minute drive home. Immediately cook plain pasta (no salt or butter). Feed child plain pasta before sugar crash.
- *The Masked Singer*, bath, iPad then bed.
- A bottle of red wine for the parent. Sleep, then repeat on Sunday.

Josh: While Rob dreads birthday parties because in his heart he doesn't like the parents of any of his daughters' friends, I absolutely love them. I am now on the Hackney four-year-old birthday party circuit and – it shames me to write – it is the most active social scene I've ever been on. My daughter goes to more parties than Tara Palmer-Tomkinson in the mid-nineties. Last summer I was knocking them out one a weekend. At one point I saw the same magician three times in six weeks, and I still loved him (to be honest, more than the kids did). I don't get what people are complaining about with kids' parties. You turn up, the children are entertained by a man who has one of those nets that makes really big bubbles and you stand at the side and talk to a dad about whether Man City need to sign a proper striker. This is living.

Rob: That's not actually true – it's more that I think it's a waste of time making friends with the parents at preschool nursery as the kids are only there for a couple of years. I completely tapped out of that. However, when they go to proper primary school you need to make an effort. We have been pretty lucky with the other parents. There was a dads' five-a-side game of football set up on a separate WhatsApp group within about two weeks of term starting. Plus we all went out for beers to be polite and meet each other, which descended into a disgusting piss-up. I remember being half-cut thinking, these are my kind of people.

Another great thing that was organised at the start of the year was a whip-round that everyone puts money into and when it comes to the birthday parties there is one good present bought from the whole class for the birthday boy/girl. This has been a revelation as it means when you inevitably forget about a birthday party you aren't scrambling around at a Wild Bean Café petrol station trying to buy a six-year-old a birthday present. Let's face it, no six-year-old wants a disposable BBQ, a litre of screen wash and a grab bag-size of roast beef Monster Munch. If the present is already sorted, it's a pressure off every weekend. Because you *will* forget your kids have been invited to birthday parties.

Josh: Then the weekend comes that it is your own child's birthday and you have to organise it. Last summer we held my daughter's birthday in the local park and because watching the local cricket team apparently isn't entertainment for four-year-olds, I had to turn up two hours early to meet the man who was putting up the soft play. He said it would be a 90-minute job – it took 17 minutes. And then he left. I was now just a man sitting alone in a park guarding a soft play. And I won't lie, it was the best Saturday of my life. Rose didn't know that while she was at home with the kids I was now just sitting in a park in the sun watching some frankly very low-level cricket from a ball pool. I opened a can of Camden Hells (classic stiff neck) and I thought, *This is happiness. After all I've been through as a parent, I deserve this.* I then spent the next 90 minutes panicking that the cricket match was too near the soft play and I was going to be responsible for a child being killed by a cricket ball. You can never really relax as a parent.

Rob: All parties need to be drop-off parties. That way, once a year, when it's your child's birthday, you have an awful day being in charge of 25 kids. But then you get free time on the other 24 weeks of the year when you are dropping off your kid. You can dump your kid at the door then sit in your car for an hour looking at Instagram, contemplating the point of life. Watching Insta stories of your happy, well-rested and fresh-faced-looking childless friends sitting in a beer garden watching the football after waking up at 10am, while you are there with a coffee-fried brain thinking about the timings of the next three parties.

Occasionally you get some parents that are sick in the head and don't allow the drop-off party so you have to go in and watch the party. I don't want to watch the party. No one wants to watch the party. The only fun part of a kids' party is seeing food that you forgot existed, like party rings and flying saucers. With one other possible highlight of watching the kids' entertainer, which is normally an Elsa impersonator, trying to explain to the birthday girl why she arrived to the party in a 2017 Vauxhall Corsa rather than by magic or on a blue ice horse. But ultimately, it's just two very loud hours of screaming, sugar highs, sugar lows and tantrums, culminating in your child crying because they don't want to go home.

No one wants 25 bad days. It's better for everyone to accept one awful day as a trade-off. It just makes sense. I don't know how to make this official or a law – do I need a petition or do I need to lobby the government? I'm sure the government has some legislation on the rules of parties.

Who Am I Any More?

*'I'm pretty sure I didn't used to be the kind
of person who would cry four times in one episode
of The Repair Shop.'*

Josh: On New Year's Eve last year we had the eternal discussion over what we should do to celebrate another terrible 12 months in the history of Western democracy and then something hit us. Why don't we just go to bed? We said it in hushed tones at first like it was a guilty secret but then the more we thought about it the better the idea became. No missing midnight because you are too pissed. No starting the year with a hangover. No reading *Funnybones* at 6am in a well of self-loathing.

So, on December 31st we went to our friends' house for dinner, had a couple of drinks and then all agreed that, to be blunt, we were exhausted and had run out of things to say to each other. We called it a night at 10pm. It was like we had hacked the system. But really what we had done was simple – we had finally admitted to ourselves who we were. We were not the people who could go out and get pissed whenever we wanted to like we used to be. We were not even parents who lied to themselves that they could live both lives. We were a middle-aged mum and dad.

And at 7am on 1 January 2022, we were the smuggest mum and dad in the UK.

Rob: The weird thing about becoming a parent is that you are given an identity at the same time as you lose all identity. You become 'Mum' or 'Dad' and everything else disappears. It's the only thing people talk to you about and the only thing you can think about. It is amazing being a dad; it's something I've always wanted to be and so I'm very fortunate that I can have children. I'm not complaining. But at the start it can feel all-consuming. Even though you have been waiting nine long months it feels like it comes out of nowhere.

During pregnancy, it's just you and your partner, who is a new shape around the mid-section. You're just wandering about, existing in this world, occasionally witnessing your partner eating some new weird shit, like Marmite on bananas. Lou's preggo craving of choice was egg-fried rice from the Chinese takeaway, but the minimum order meant she had to buy four portions every time. Which meant we always had a fridge full of rice, but we were blissfully happy living this new rice-dominated lifestyle. Then bang! This little gremlin appears requiring food, water, clothing, shelter and care, 24/7. For the first-time parent it's overwhelming. It's the only thing on your mind every second of every day. Are they okay? Am I doing this okay? Are people watching? Am I doing it wrong? Will I be able to provide for the next 18 years? Why do they shit so much even though they only have tiny bottles of milk? The maths simply doesn't add up...

Josh: Perhaps the greatest impact parenthood has had on my life is it has made me an emotional mess. The other day we were sorting through my daughter's old books, as my son is now the age where we can read him *Each Peach Pear Plum* and he can look at it blankly. Putting those books on the shelf, remembering each one that I had read to my daughter as she had grown into a four-year-old girl, I found myself unable to stop crying as I considered that the time in my life when I read her the frankly overrated *Goodnight Moon* had gone forever. It was a pathetic sight, a man crying into a copy of *Fox's Socks*, only stopping the tears by telling himself he was going to get to experience that all again with his son. (But then that will be it. I absolutely do not need to do this a third time.)

It isn't just my children's reading material that sets me off. Since becoming a parent I have become emotionally vulnerable to everything I encounter. I'm pretty sure I didn't used to be the kind of person who would cry four times in one episode of *The Repair Shop*. While I like to consider myself a modern man who appreciates that you need to engage your own emotions, it would be useful to be able to get through a TV show about a man mending a rocking horse with sentimental value without crying like a First World War widow.

There is a cliché of the dad as an emotionally unavailable and distant figure of authority. Absolutely no worries here, mate. If anything I am far too emotionally available. I tell my daughter I love her so often I know it is getting a little oppressive and, to be honest, needy. In 30 years she will be talking to her therapist about how her dad maybe just needed to be a bit colder, it was all a bit much.

But don't worry, in other ways I have transitioned into the

classic dad, fulfilling all the tropes of dads before me. I have a set of Allen keys in the kitchen drawer. If someone asks me about buying a car I offer the advice to buy second-hand, adding 'you lose £2,000 the moment you have driven it off the forecourt'. I try and see how far we can get into winter without putting the heating on. I am the owner of a car with those weird sun guards on the back windows. In short, I am middle-aged. I have lost my edge and I am fine with that.

Rob: As they get older they sleep better, are more self-sufficient and, crucially, out of the house at school, allowing you to claw back some time for yourself. You will find yourself in your empty house completely alone in total silence. You will stand there and realise this hasn't happened in four and a half years. It might freak you out at first – you don't know how to act. You can shout at the top of your voice without the fear of waking up your kids. My children sleep like logs now but it still says on my Deliveroo delivery instructions 'please knock quietly, new baby sleeping' – an instruction I punched into my phone after the loudest man in the world screamed, 'I've got four portions of egg-fried rice for you again,' through his helmet on my doorstep, waking up my newborn baby.

You might start to think, hold on, I've got all this free time but I've forgotten what I like. I don't know what I do in my spare time any more because I've not had any for so long. That's what happened to me. I first noticed this when I was alone in the house and went on my Sky TV planner to watch something I had recorded. I had nothing recorded. NOTHING. Just a sea of *Bluey*, *Peppa Pig* and *Octonauts*. So I just sat and stared at a blank screen thinking, *What did I used to do?* I remembered one thing, but once I'd had a wank I couldn't think of anything else. After that furious three minutes I sat there thinking, *I'm sure I had some hobbies and things I liked before I was Dad.*

Josh: I am terrified about time passing. I have a friend whose children have grown up and he told me that he has boxes of old photos of their childhoods that he can't ever dare to look at as it would make him too sad. I can't stop thinking about this day arriving. The truth is having children is both the fastest and slowest time will ever travel, on one hand losing years of their lives as the baby you held in your arms has suddenly transformed into a teenager; on the other hand each sleepless night feeling slower and more never-ending than the reign of a Tory government. This means I find myself wishing time away or begging it to stop depending on the minute of the day. Desperately dreaming of the moment when she will finally put her shoes on as we are already late for nursery and then worrying about the day she will no longer fit in those shoes and I'll have to put them in a memory box I will always be too scared to look in.

Rob: For me, one of the best things about having kids is the appreciation of time. Having kids makes you realise how much time there is in a day. If they wake up at 5am you could have breakfast, a snack, lunch, *Frozen and Frozen II* back to back, a trip to the park and back in the garden for the paddling pool by 11am. That is totally doable – parents reading will agree and non-parents will think I'm talking bullshit. I've been walking down the road after an early start with the kids and someone will say, 'Good morning.' I'll look at them in shock and disbelief, thinking to myself there is no way it can still be morning. Jesus Christ, eight hours until bedtime. I've still got another full day in the office to go of childcare. Older generations don't understand, they all think we are over-sensitive, over-protective woke snowflakes. Sure, some of us are – naming no names, Josh Widdicombe. But it was easier for parents in the '70s and '80s as they only looked after their kids until they were about four, and then they just got let outside to play with the other kids. We can't do that with our kids in 2022; the roads are too busy with cars and perverts.

We complain about having no time as parents but look at how much you can do in one full day. Our brains run on fear and anxiety and are always telling us to hurry up, there isn't enough time, we've got to do 'this and that', because if we don't do 'this and that' then 'this and that' will happen. Blah, blah, blah. It never stops; there's always a new 'this and that' consuming us with worry as parents. It's a constant noise of thoughts, unrelenting and exhausting. And while this is going on in your head, a four-year-old is asking where her Mr Horny Triceratops teddy is.

I think it's good to realise that we are filling the time with unnecessary thoughts complicating every moment. There is space and moments for quiet reflection in everything that we do if we slow down and notice it. If you just stop thinking for a moment and fully experience what's going on in that exact moment you realise how much time there is.

If you don't believe me then try this. Stop reading this book now and look out of the nearest window for a full minute. Don't panic, it's not going to go full self-help cult leader wanker. Trust me there will be a dick joke just around the corner. Look out of the nearest window at a tree or a cloud in the sky for 60 seconds non-stop. Focusing on the tree/cloud and not thinking about 'this and that' on your to-do list. If you do it for a full 60 seconds, I promise you it will feel like a two-week holiday. It might take a few attempts but give it a good go. I just tried to do it and looked at my stopwatch after 13 seconds. A truly pathetic attempt. But just by sitting and doing nothing for one minute it makes you realise how long time is and how much we have. It's really calming and relaxing if you surrender to it.

I find when I do these little 60-second mini breaks from my life, when I eventually go back to whatever task I'm trying to complete, whether it be parenting or my job, I approach it in a calmer and more considered way. I sometimes do it on stage – though obviously not for a full minute as that would be a disaster in a comedy show. But if I feel like I'm rushing or my words are getting away from me, I'll say nothing for two or three seconds. I will sit with the quietness and it will reset me before I go again with another joke about the size of my teeth. Your brain will hate it; it wants you to keep moving and keep planning to stay safe from predators. That's why it's so hard to do nothing but sit still and breathe. The brain would rather you spent that minute scrolling on Instagram or a YouTube vortex binge. So it takes a bit of training, but if you can stop yourself to do nothing for 60 seconds when you're getting worked up it can really help.

Before I became a dad, I didn't really have enough hobbies and interests to fill 24 hours. But I was excellent at filling time with stuff just for the sake of filling time because we have so much time to fill. I didn't realise what I was doing because it crept up on me as a teenager and in my twenties. But once I had a kid all that time-filling crap had to stop because it was all hands on deck with the baby. But now the kids are in school and I have this time back. So now when I'm not working or parenting I do a lot of just sitting and staring and I fucking love it. It started off in 60-second bursts but has started creeping up to 30 minutes. Sometimes in silence or sometimes with music or a calming voice on my headphones. I now find thinking of something to do is exhausting. I love just sitting and doing nothing, although sometimes I have the telly on in the background so I don't look mental. But I'm not watching it. I'm just sitting there with nothing in my brain and it's great. Obviously on the hour, every hour I will masturbate. But that's normal, isn't it? The 'cuckoo cock' I call it.

Josh: I do worry that in a way, being a parent has swallowed my identity. I had planned never to do comedy about my child. Now I am writing the spin-off book of a podcast about being a parent. I parent and then go upstairs to talk about being a parent, interview someone about being a parent or write about being a parent. The problem is you are left with no gaps in your life, so, like Rob, I don't know what to do when suddenly I have time on my hands. Did I used to watch TV? Did I cook an actual meal with ingredients you had to buy separately in a shop? Did I play golf? Surely 'looking at your phone' isn't a hobby.

It excites me that one day I will again have the freedom to do these things (not the cooking, I will never do that again now Deliveroo exists). In fact, I already have a list of things in my head that I am going to do when my children grow up and I suddenly have time to myself again:

1. Go on European city breaks to every major capital
2. Watch Plymouth Argyle home and away
3. Learn to play golf
4. Finally do that Wikipedia podcast

I know as time goes on my children will pull away and have their own lives and I will have to try to be fine with that. But I also know I won't be fine with it; I will be completely unable to deal with it and all the things I now dream of being able to do will not make up for it. At the moment I can only imagine having the time to go and watch Plymouth Argyle on a Saturday, but in ten years I will be sitting on the train back from a 1–0 defeat to Rotherham thinking, I wish I was reading *Fox's Socks*.

INTERLUDE 5

Non-Parenting Hell

Sadly the most popular voice on our podcast is our producer Michael, a man without children who has to listen to us talk about children for two hours a week. Here, by popular demand, he answers questions from our listeners about what he makes of it all.

When Rob and Josh first asked me to contribute to the *Parenting Hell* book, I was both honoured and flattered to be even just a small part of what will undoubtedly be a work of seminal literary brilliance, the like of which I truly believe English literature curricula will study decades from now alongside Shakespeare, Wordsworth and, at this rate, Richard Osman. (Hi, Richard. We'd love to have you on the podcast so the door is, and always will be, very much open...)

I very quickly realised that they were both just really busy/ lazy (delete as appropriate) and this was a shortcut to bumping up the word count. A prouder man would have walked away and told them to pad out their own vanity project. But it's either this or go back to working on comedy panel shows, so I swallowed what's left of my dignity and got typing...

My next thought was, as a man with no children of his own, what could I really contribute to the subject? And was I in danger of becoming hated by hundreds of thousands of listeners as I inconsiderately stumbled around these pages talking about a life of late weekend brunches, impromptu foreign city breaks and hours upon hours of sleep?

And then somebody had the idea that it should be a Q and A, where the listeners submitted questions for me to answer about the podcast and anything and everything beyond...

So here we are... you asked, I've answered.

Joe: As a non-parent, what's the most eye-opening thing about looking after a child for a friend or family member?

How utterly relentless it is. I don't think as a non-parent you can ever really understand the level of exhaustion involved. I recently took one of my nieces to London Zoo for the day, and I should caveat, I absolutely adore her and she's one of my favourite people in the world, and I love spending time with her. But being responsible for answering every question, every decision, every irrational or illogical bit of behaviour, making sure they don't accidentally climb into the lion enclosure (she didn't) or deliberately try and grab a meerkat (she did) was like the world's most insane endurance test. Like a Tough Mudder but with a stage where you have to cut up someone's food into small chunks and then wage a psychological war on why they need to eat the freshly-cut vegetables and not the Kinder Egg that right now you don't even have the ability to procure even if your life depended on it. It's the relentless irrationality that grinds you down. They say the key to winning an argument is not being right, it's convincing the other person that you're right. Whoever wrote that has never had to deal with an exhausted, overheated child having a meltdown in the middle of a toy shop while shouting 'You're not my dad!' as increasingly concerned security guards start to advance on your position among the *Star Wars* Lego.

At the end of that day I was so physically and mentally exhausted I fell asleep on the sofa watching *Moana* with her several hours before my usual bedtime. And then I was rudely awakened by her giggling while drawing more beard hair on my face with a Sharpie pen as she thought my current beard, and I quote, 'made me look like someone who was sad and lonely a lot of the time'. I don't know if that's a criticism of the quality of my facial hair, or just a vibe of general existential malaise she was picking up on? Both of which aren't without merit. Out of the mouths of babes, as they say...

It wasn't until the following morning I also realised she'd given me large patches of blue ink-coloured hair for similar reasons. So as eye-openers go, if one 12-hour shift with a six-year-old was enough to incapacitate me to that degree, heaven knows what a week, a month or even years of decimated sleep would do to my spirits and competence as a functioning human. I have nothing but the utmost respect and admiration for all the fatigued, walking dead parents out there in the trenches fighting the good fight day after exhausting day.

Finn, Cambridge: Which of the boys has less of an understanding of technology?

I'd say Josh. He's so stuck in the 1990s he insists on using a dial-up internet connection rather than high-speed broadband, which can obviously cause a bit of an issue recording the podcast at times. We once had to stop recording mid-episode because Rose needed to use the landline and the 56k modem was tying up the line. What's even worse is he insists on only being contacted via beeper as he views WhatsApp with the same scepticism as a conspiracy theorist does the footage of the Moon landing. If the episode is ever up later than expected on a Tuesday or Friday, I want you all to know it's because Josh didn't get to a payphone to call me back about an important matter after I'd sent him a 343 or 911 message code.

Claire, Hong Kong: As someone who isn't surrounded by tiny terrorists, what's the one piece of parenting advice that you've heard repeated on the podcast, but think it's utter rubbish?

That it gets easier. As an objective observer, the level and power of deniability in that statement every time it is uttered by a guest always makes me smile. Both parties want to believe it. Both parties NEED to believe it. It's a coping mechanism. And I totally understand why as either the person in the eye of the parenting storm, or as the lighthouse guiding the way on a stormy sea of fractured and exhausted existential turmoil, you would tell someone it gets better and buy into it yourself. It's about survival. But from the outside and with no skin in the game it seems like a complete fallacy. It doesn't get easier. It just gets different. Or if you want a motivational quote for your fridge magnet or tasteless wall stencil, 'it doesn't get easier, you get better at it'.

Charles: If Rob and Josh's kids got into the classic 'my dad could beat up your dad' argument, who wins the fight?

Rob. No question. I don't think in more than ten years I've ever seen Josh raise his voice in any state of rage or potential violence. He's a man who admirably avoids any kind of conflict, and therefore I think would be a disaster in a fight. He'd probably end up hurting himself.

Whereas Rob grew up with a clan of older brothers so has taken some licks in his formative years. That kind of conditioning doesn't leave you, even if the reflexes get a bit rusty as you enter stiff neck territory in later life. But the ability to light that fuse is always there. So I'd predict Rob by TKO within the first round. And if anyone from Matchroom Boxing or the UFC is reading this, let's talk. I think a 'Rob vs. Josh' *Parenting Hell* pay-per-view charity boxing match would have more of a cultural imprint than the 'Rumble in the Jungle' and the 'Thrilla in Manila' combined.

Lucy, Derbyshire: Who, out of Rob and Josh, would you marry?

That's really tricky. Obviously both great guys, loving husbands and fathers, but I'm not sure who would be the most compatible with me. I think Josh would be the more tender lover. And we'd not be short of things to discuss. But the constant worrying might get a bit much for me every day. Whereas Rob and I have very similar backgrounds, so there would be an easy shorthand there, but it could also just devolve into a bareback, working-class, alpha-dog fuck fest. Like *Mad Max Beyond Thunderdome*. Two working-class boys go in, one comes out.

I think ultimately I'd move to Salt Lake City and marry them both. Split my time so it wasn't the same meal every night. We all get the best of each other and live happily ever after. Like when you go to Häagen-Dazs for some ice cream, you never get two scoops of the same flavour. Unless you're a sociopath. In fact, I usually get three flavours in a waffle cone so I might see if Elis James fancies a new life out in Utah to complete the gang. Spend our weekends in a big 1990s football circle jerk. I'm not sure what would happen to the podcast as a result, but I believe love would prevail.

Natalie: **Dear sexy-voiced Michael, as a child-free man, which part of parenting makes you want to double-wrap with condoms?**

Sleep. The lack of sleep. The relentless, soul-crushing, life-sucking lack of sleep which, with the exception of one or two questionable methods, every single guest has stated as a massive issue. And an issue without any real guaranteed solution.

It's one of the genuine miracles of evolution and procreation that the known side effects of having children are there for all to see, and the cautionary tales are passed down from generation to generation like a family heirloom, but instead of an antique watch or an ugly piece of crockery, your parents and grandparents regale you with tales that sound not dissimilar to traumatic bouts of PTSD, and yet we do it anyway. And then a great many do it again. And again. (No judgement.)

But if you said to me outside of parenting, do you want to have an experience – parts of which will be amazing, we just can't guarantee how, when or why – but you'll also never sleep properly again, it will strain your relationship in ways you can't even begin to imagine, and it will virtually bankrupt you, I suspect I'd pass up the chance. In fact, I'd openly say you're out of your tiny mind and you really need to work on the marketing and PR angle of this red-letter day dumpster fire you're pitching me. It sounds like hell. Parenting hell. Someone should make a podcast about it.

***Kirsty, Baldock:* There are loads of activities out there but you have to have a child to do them (otherwise you look a bit weird). For example, Digger World is somewhere I really want to go but need a child. If there's one activity that you would love to do, without judgement, what would it be and why?**

I think it's probably Legoland, but only if there are also no other children there. And I'd follow it up with the holy trinity of a game of Laser Quest and a McDonald's Happy Meal (probably two and see if I can convince the staff to switch out the duplicate toy. Something I tried and failed endlessly to do as a kid. I can see a whole box of them behind you!! Just swap it out, you jobsworth!).

Gemma: What's the most stressful part of your life with no kids?

Most days it's deciding what to have for dinner. Or what film to watch in the evening completely uninterrupted. Sorry.

Charlotte: Be brutally honest, who would you rather have as a dad, Rob or Josh, and why?

All joking aside, I think they're both brilliant parents and I have nothing but immense respect and admiration for what they (and Lou and Rose of course!) do and the way they do it. It would be an honour to have either of them as a dad.

Ruth: How much time do you spend editing the podcast?

A ratio of about 5 to 1.

So if we record for an hour it takes about five hours from start to release into the wild. There's lots of boring stiff-neck technical stuff that happens in there as well, but when a guest drones on about something I know will never make the edit (no names mentioned) then I can rapidly feel my day and sometimes evening slipping away before my very eyes...

Rob and Josh of course are consummate professionals and require almost no producing or editing in any way shape or form. You could basically just put the show out live and there would be no drop in quality and we definitely wouldn't get cancelled or sued.

Jen, Staines: **If and when you have a child, who out of Rob and Josh would you ask to babysit and why?**

It would depend on the amount of time and frequency. If it was just a couple of hours on a date night, I'd probably go with Rob as a babysitter, knowing full well we'd be returning to hyped-up children, who even if they hadn't been pumped full of sugar and E numbers, were in such a manic state of giddiness they may as well have been mainlining soft drinks and racking up lines of Haribo. But the good thing about Rob as a babysitter is that I think they'd have a great time and, most importantly, I don't think outside of a serious maiming that I'd get a call because something had gone wrong or they wouldn't behave. I think he's got it in his locker to free-form his way out of any situation, even if they weren't his kids.

With Josh, I think I'd be far more likely to get a text or call because my child had a mini meltdown over something relatively small; he'd overthink it and end up calling us because he was worried about something that I hadn't even considered.

Amber: **If you had to picture babysitting Rob and Josh's children for the day, how do you think it would go?**

For me? Great. For the kids, great. For Rob and Lou and Josh and Rose when they returned? Possibly not so great. They don't call me the Child Whisperer for nothing and it would be difficult for them to parent with any degree of respect or competency after the children have experienced a true master at work. Like when Ole Gunnar Solskjaer took over at Manchester United, the spectre of Alex Ferguson's legacy and genius loomed large.

One day of babysitting with producer Michael and they'd be insisting on a statue outside the house. Being the cool uncle with absolute disregard for any consequences is the dream job when it comes to your friends' and family's children.

Kat: If you could choose any guest for the podcast, who would it be?

Elton John. Obama. Alex Ferguson. The Holy Trinity. If any of them listen, we'd love to have you. (Or if anyone can hook us up with them, please do.)

Please note we do only record from 10am to 1pm on a Monday though, so you'll need to clear your diary for us. Rob and Josh are very particular about how much work they are willing to do and three hours a week in that pre-designated slot is the absolute maximum before the union is on my back and I'm frantically rummaging for Acaster and Gamble's numbers to see if they are planning on having kids. I'm not saying Rob and Josh have become podcast divas in the last two years, I'm just not NOT saying that either.

And Finally, We'll End on This...

Josh: Rose and I spent the first few months of being parents heading towards various imaginary deadlines, the times when it would get easier and suddenly those sleepless nights would be worth it. Just get through the first six weeks, the sleep regression, teething, hand, foot and mouth... and then we realised, oh wait, this never ends. There's no land of milk and honey when life is easy. It will be unbelievably tough in different ways for the next 18 years (minimum). In a way, that is the best thing a child can teach you: that place you think you are heading, where you can relax and life will be perfect, it doesn't exist. So enjoy the here and now, because this is it.

But let's be honest, despite the nappy rash, sleepless nights and having to talk to Rob Beckett for two hours a week – having children is brilliant. I know we have tried not to say that in this book because no one wants to sit on a sun lounger reading about people enjoying their lives but, really, off the record between us, being a parent is the best thing I have ever done. And I have been on *Celebrity Tipping Point*.

Rob: Of course there are points when parenting is a complete and utter ball ache and we have covered that extensively in this book. But no one wants to hear about the amazing parts of being a parent and more crucially it's almost impossible to articulate those special moments. It's almost like a spiritual airy fairy exchange of energy that words cannot describe. In a world dominated by social media, money and success, the truth is the things that really matter and mean something can't be ranked with numbers and statistics. It's only the shallow stuff that needs numbers to show you a warped sense of 'worth'. How much money do you have? How many followers do you have? How many BAFTAs have you won? How many books have you sold? All the stuff that doesn't matter has numbers attached. When I'm lying on the sofa and one of my girls comes up and cuddles next to me and falls asleep, it trumps everything else. It's a priceless moment that money or success cannot even come close to replicate. There is no price you can pay for a child to say, 'I love you, Daddy.' It's not for sale. It's impossible to make that relationship available for purchase.

It's the same as motivation, loyalty or love: it's free and only there if you put the effort in. You can buy a Ferrari, you can earn £100,000 a year, you can have a million Instagram followers, but you cannot buy or hashtag 'gifted' those special connections you have with your children. The feeling you get when you see them go off to their first day of school, sitting with them as they open their exam results, having their first legal drink with them at 18, waving them off on their first driving lesson, meeting their first boyfriend or girlfriend, walking them down the aisle, and holding their firstborn with your new name 'Grandad' – all these things about being a parent bring a special energy to life that goes way beyond anything you thought you wanted. I am so lucky to be a dad and in spite of the challenges it's the best thing about my life. If my life was stripped away from me, everything had to go, house, money, car, job, being a dad and my kids would be the one thing I would be left clinging onto. As well as my fully completed Euro '96 sticker book. Oh yeah, and Lou.

Josh: If writing this book has taught me anything (and let's be honest, there is every chance it hasn't) then it is that the things that stay with you as a parent are not the big events – the first birthday, the removal of stabilisers from the bike – but the small, inconsequential moments that catch you off guard and you cherish and mythologise about your child's life forever. There is a reason that our parents talked about the time Rob fell off a table or me refusing to play with girls in a WI hut, that Rob decided to write 1,000 words on places his daughters have been sick but had nothing to say about their first teeth. These are the things you remember, the tiny details that make you thankful that looking after these two little children that get up at 6am every day is the thing that consumes your life, even if it is at the sacrifice of Saturday mooching.

As I write this, I can hear my daughter playing with her best friend in the next room; they are discussing a teddy bear that is called Robbie, despite the fact I doubt my daughter has ever even met a Robbie as it isn't 1998. Listening to them talking, trying to work out the world with four-year-old logic is making my heart ache in a way that I didn't know was possible before becoming a father. Who knew there was a feeling stronger than talking to the girl you fancy but knew you would never ask out at school?

Rob: It's the same for me, the little moments that make it feel so special. My daughters now know how to work the TV remote on their own without my help. It's fucking glorious.

Josh: When we started the podcast as *Lockdown Parenting Hell* (before the Opal Fruits to Starburst rebrand) we saw it as a way of letting off steam, venting about the situation we were in. While no one wants to hear anyone talk about lockdown ever again, it is worth noting that it was a time more than any other that highlighted the differences between the lives of those with and without children. We parents didn't learn Spanish, get into baking or spend our mornings dripping sweat onto our coffee table in the company of Joe Wicks – we just tried to get through the days under house arrest with our child and mental health intact. Seething with anger at anyone without children who dared to complain about being locked in.

It didn't help that, at this time, it felt everyone on social media had taken a global pandemic and turned it into a yoga retreat. Maybe the reason people responded to *Parenting Hell* was that it was honest, it showed a life so many of us are living, holding on by our fingertips looking after children that won't sleep when you stroke their nose and won't eat unless you remove all flavour from the food on their plate. We may not be able to give you useful tips on how to discipline your child, but we were able to offer what all parents need: reassurance that everyone finds it just as tough as you.

I have always worried about the name *Parenting Hell*, partly because I'm the kind of person who can worry about anything and partly because parenting isn't hell. Sometimes it is, and the good news for me and Rob is these are the funniest bits, the kind of things you include in a book. Recording our podcast and writing this book has come to be a place for us to unload these lowest moments. *Parenting Hell* has become an outlet for us, a cathartic experience passed off as entertainment. We are lucky in what we get to do. When I am cleaning up fox shit on my doorstep, I can think, well at least I can talk about this on the podcast. If we didn't have the podcast I would just be a man cleaning up fox shit.

Rob: I'm personally really excited to hear the fox shit story on the next episode of the podcast. I've always had the sense Josh felt uncomfortable with the name 'Parenting Hell' but I think it's fine. Mainly because life is hell and parenting is just another part of life. Life is so difficult, there's so much to do and see and there are people everywhere reminding you of how much there is to do and see. Most people in the world wake up in the morning with the thought, *Oh, fucking hell. I've got to do that today*. Whether you are a parent or not. Life is really tough and we are all doing really well getting through each day with a certain level of sanity intact. We have lots of listeners with children but also lots of listeners without, because life is hard and it's made easier listening to other people finding it hard.

I love doing the podcast and I loved writing this book. I'm a big fan of honesty and I have been as honest as humanly possible in your headphones and on these pages. I think the only way to get through life is to cut the shit and stop pretending everything is perfect. Be honest, embrace your imperfections and laugh about them and then you are halfway there getting through the day. I feel better after every podcast episode we record as offloading your worries and stresses to a friend is so important.

Josh: And to end on some honesty, that just about concludes everything we know about parenting. We hope it has been of some help to you. Thank God that we didn't back up Rob's hubris in the first meeting and try and get a three-book deal; to quote Rob on the phone to me just now, 'the well is dry'. It turns out we had exactly a book's worth of experiences worth committing to paper.

Rob: Maybe one day we will write another book when our kids are older and we can tell you about the hell of the teenage years or maybe we will do another book when Josh has his third kid.

Josh: I'm not going to have a third kid.

Rob: Of course you are.

Josh: No, I'm genuinely not.

Rob: Keep telling yourself that.

Josh: I'm not telling myself anything, it's a fact.

Rob: Course it is.

Josh: It is.

AND FINALLY, WE'LL END ON THIS...

Rob: It's not.

Josh: It is.

Rob: Don't you think you will regret this when your third kid reads it?

Josh: They won't as I'm not having a third kid.

Rob: You are.

Josh: I'm not.

Rob: Think of it this way, we need it for the next book...

Acknowledgements

Rob: Thank you to my darling wife and mother to my beautiful two girls. Lou is the better parent, person and writer. I'll be out of a job soon and I'm looking forward to Lou's first full book, where she can properly stick the boot in.

Thank you to my beautiful daughters for providing so much content from swallowing coins to writing 'piss' on the wall twice. I love you more than anything. Your little cheeky faces light up the room and my entire life. You've made everything better. I feel like the luckiest man in the world to have three such amazing women I can call my little family.

Big up my parents, Sue and Dave, for always being there to help with the kids whenever we need them. Also, for all the great and sometimes questionable advice you give us. Michael and Teresa, who have also been so helpful and supportive with childcare. My girls are so blessed to have four such amazing and caring grandparents.

ACKNOWLEDGEMENTS

Also thank you to Josh for laughing at all my jokes on
the podcast, even the shit ones. You've got my back and I've
got yours.

Josh: There isn't enough thanks in the world for Rose. You
are by far the most patient, selfless and best-dressed parent
I have ever met. More importantly we used to have a real
laugh before the kids came along, I'm sure of it. Most of all,
thank you for laughing rather than leaving me when I said I
had read Rob's bits and I worried he was far nicer about Lou
than I was about you. You know I'm just bad at expressing
positive emotions.

To my two kids, I can't tell you how much I love you and
want to experience every moment of your childhood, between
the hours of 7am and 7pm. I hope you enjoy this book one day
in about 30 years.

To the world's most chilled-out parents, Tom and Sarah, you
taught me not to take life too seriously and not to respect any
figure of authority, which is a gamble for parents. I couldn't
have asked for a more perfect upbringing.

And thank you to Sam, Shell, Clarey Poppins, the staff
at Rosemary Works East and everyone who has ever helped
look after our kids at some point, even for an hour: you
prevented our inevitable divorce and did a much better job
than I ever could.

Finally, from both of us: Danny Julian, Flo Howard,
Rich McCann, Lily Morris, Joe Norris, Ann Kennedy and
everyone else at Off The Kerb, who are all first and foremost
good-hearted and hardworking people. It's just a bonus that

they are also the best comedy managers and promoters in the world.

And thank you to Matthew Phillips, Madiya Altaf, Emily Rough, Stephen Dumughn, Karen Stretch, Liz Marvin, Ali Nazari, Lizzie Dorney-Kingdom and everyone at Bonnier for taking a huge punt on something that could really not have worked.

Thank you to Michael for listening to us drone on about our kids and edit out at least two things a week that would end our careers. And thank you to all the guests for coming on to the podcast purely in exchange for us pretending we have read and enjoyed their new books.

Most of all, thank you to the listeners (and now readers) for taking a lockdown hobby and making it one of the first things that'll be mentioned in our obituaries. We genuinely love doing the podcast and find it so thrilling and touching that so many of you listen every week. You made lockdown and beyond easier for us and I hope in some way we returned the favour.

Bonus Material:
Parenting Tips

Rob's Tips

- Never rush a shit.

- Get a dog *after* kids, otherwise you will treat it like a baby and it will be a little needy bastard when the kids come along.

- If possible, move near family, friends, anyone that will help with childcare. It's better to live somewhere crap with help and support than somewhere amazing alone.

- You don't need to buy and build a cot until your kid is about six months old. Obviously you will need a Moses basket or something similar.

- The smaller the buggy the better. You don't need a massive Range Rover size one. Your kids aren't as precious as you think they are. Look how busy the Tube is – humans are tough bastards.

- Don't give in on the naming. Both parents need to believe in the name 100 per cent or it will haunt you forever.

- Don't bother with a holiday abroad until they are four. Save your money and go somewhere top-level when they are older and you all get to enjoy it.

- Before you have children, be careful what you say about parents who give their kids iPads at the table in restaurants.

Those words will come back into your face as a giant egg after you've had a giant slice of humble pie.

- Booking a babysitter for the hangover in the morning is just as important as booking the babysitter for the night out.

- If possible, take shifts. If the kid is being a prick in the night and won't sleep, if one of you does 11pm to 3am and the other does 3am to 7am, then at least you're getting some sleep. There's no point in you both being up all night.

- Avoid paddling pools at all costs. It just turns into a disgusting pond of filth and ruins your grass. Running through the sprinkler is the perfect combo on a summer's day. Kids love it, it's less dangerous for non-swimmers and it waters the grass.

Josh's Tips

- Being the hider in hide and seek is a great way to get 45 seconds alone looking at your phone.

- Get one of those heatproof cups that weird camping people drink their tea from. Otherwise you will be drinking exclusively cold tea you forgot you made 45 minutes ago for the first two years.

- Never let your child see an episode of *Peppa Pig* – there is no way back.

- Live near your parents; it is the greatest form of free babysitting. I don't live near mine.

- Always remember that over-competitive parents are fragile people trying to make sense of their own insecurities and the biggest wankers you can meet.

- If your child sleeps well, never, ever, ever tell another parent. You will rightly be blacklisted from all social occasions and parenting WhatsApp groups.

- These are all the tips I have, sorry. I have nothing else useful to offer. And crucially, unlike Rob, I don't think I have this thing nailed.